HEALING the RAGE WITHIN

How I overcame my inner rage after being sexually abused and raped.

Author Photo/Cover Design by: Eboni D Brewster

Copyright © 2013 by Yuoranda Walker

All rights reserved. No part of this book may be reproduced in any form or by any means without prior written permission from the publisher.

HEALING the RAGE WITHIN

How I overcame my inner rage after being sexually abused and raped.

Yuoranda L. Walker

Dedication

First and foremost I dedicate this book to the Most High because it is only HIS doing that I am able to truthfully and shamelessly share my story with the world. It is only because of HIM, that I am able to forgive those who trespassed against me, forgive myself, Heal My Hurt and call myself a survivor.

I dedicate this book to my wonderful husband, Aaron J. Walker, who has supported me from the beginning. Writing & reliving my past was hurtful and hard, but through it all you were my rock and I am forever grateful for your strength. You are forever my King, and I love you.

I dedicate this book to my three wonderful, awesome, inspiring children, Dj, Eboni, & Myles. You three have cheered me on, encouraged me, and most of all inspired me to share my truth. You gave me my space when it was crunch time and you kept me company when I needed to laugh and feel young again. I love you all.

I dedicate this book to my close friends & family who understood my need to share my truth and supported me in so many ways. You all prayed with me & for me as well as kept me encouraged to continue to write and never give up. You gave me hope that many will be touched & inspired by reading my story and for that alone…for the hope, I thank you from my heart and I love you all to life. (Cedric & Marcia H, Romona D, Krystal D, Kewana G, Sharon W, Esther J, Tracy B)

I dedicate this book to two women who have been like my mothers for the past 6 years. Since I moved to Houston & we started working together, you two have helped me tremendously. When I had nothing, you stepped in and shared what you had. You prayed for me and mine, you kept me encouraged, you helped me find & figure out a way, when all my eyes saw was no way. You did not allow me to give up. You expected greatness from me just as if I was your very own child and I dared to not disappoint. You believed in me and when I think about what I have endured, all I hear are your voices telling me to pray and not give up. Mrs. Linda K & Mrs. Jessie F, I thank you for your guidance, prayers, love, sternness, and kindness and I love you to life.

I dedicate this book to the ones who hurt me, the ones who failed to protect me, the ones who took from me the one thing I fought so hard and so long to get back… MY PEACE WITHIN. I pray that one day, you are able to ask the Most High for forgiveness and you are able to forgive yourself for the trespasses you did against me. Now because I know that there is no big sin/little sin and I know that we ALL sin…including myself…If I have done any wrong towards you, I beg your forgiveness & I NEED you to know that I forgive you and I love you.

Last but certainly not least…

I dedicate this book to ALL the survivors of child sexual abuse, rape, & domestic violence. If you made it through, then you have SURVIVED and now you MUST began the process to *Heal Your Hurt*. It will not be easy and you will want to give up, but I beg you, PUSH THROUGH!!! Your healing, your peace of mind, & your sanity is all for you. Holding on to your anger, hurt, pain, rage & low self esteem hurts you and those who truly love & care for you. Healing is your right and you deserve it!!

Heal Your Hurt

Table of Contents

Introduction:

Part 1: Lord, Why Me?

Part 2: A Raging War on the Inside

Part 3: Healing the RAGE

Part 4: A New Me

About the Author:

Introduction

This is My Story…My Truth as I lived it everyday. These are my personal thoughts, actions, & reactions towards the abuse and rape that I endured in my childhood and adulthood. This is my pain that I carried for years deep in my soul. This is my anger, my hurt, my tears, and my RAGE that I almost allowed to take me out as I allowed it to overtake me. This is my healing journey, my self discovery, my willingness to call the truth the truth regardless of how hard it was or how much it hurt me. This is My True Story of how I was able to stop living with a victim mentality because of what I endured and began living in survivorship because of what I endured.

This book was not written to bring guilt nor shame upon any of the people who hurt me, failed to protect me or (as I believed) turned their backs on me. This book was not written to place me in a seat above the rest to look down low. The purpose of me putting pen to paper to write *Healing the Rage Within* is because I want to help other women, who have endured the same, understand the importance of healing as well as encourage them to do the work to begin their own healing journey.

Having to take myself back to being a helpless victim was hard and painful. It brought me pain and tears but it also brought me joy. Joy in knowing that I have overcome & I am a survivor. I am a survivor of the abuse, the rape, but most importantly I am a survivor of the rage that held me in bondage for years.

I hope you, the reader, can read my story free of judgment. I hope you can take my words and apply them to your situation…no matter where the hurt came from. I hope you get the BIG picture that I attempted to color between the covers of this book.

Heal Your Hurt!

This Page Intentionally Left Blank

Part 1: Lord, Why Me?

I remember the day as if it were just yesterday. I don't remember my exact age but we (my mom, two brothers, my stepdad and I) were staying with my grandmother for a short time before our move. My mother and stepfather were active duty military and we were on our way to live in another country, England to be exact. I remember being excited about going to another country, meeting different people, eating different foods and learning a different language. I was as excited as any young child would be. I mean not many children I knew had the opportunity to travel the world. I remember telling my cousins and my friends and they joined in on my excitement, but that excitement was very short lived for me. The day was a regular one, nothing to get excited about. Mom and Joe were fussing about something and the fussing turned into fighting. This was their usual routine, so I didn't think much of it. Actually I remember thinking, "Go on, fight and get it over with."

Most young children would have been scared, but not me. Like I said, it was routine for us. It was something we witnessed on a regular basis and for a child, it was my norm and I had grown immune to this disease. I have no idea what they were fighting for. All I remember about it was being outside, them fighting and my grandmother trying to break it up as my brothers and I stood by and watched. I recall mom saying something about going to a hotel after the fighting was over and I remember asking her if I could go. She said no, and without looking back got in the car and left.

Mommy (my grandmother) was a nurse and worked at night. She had to get to work and I remember her fussing about all the chaos that was caused. She told my stepdad that he would sleep in her room with my younger brother, I was to sleep in the middle room and my oldest brother was to sleep in the back room. Mommy left and the night went on as if nothing had ever happened. My brothers & I still joked around and we still watched TV with my stepfather. We still ate dinner, bathed and kissed him good night…just as we had done every night. I honestly don't recall anything special or exciting happening. I also don't recall actually going to bed, but I know I did. I remember being asleep in the middle room but waking up upon hearing the bedroom door open. Because we (the grandchildren) had heard so many ghost stories about the 'middle room' and strange things happening on my grandmother's property, when the bedroom door opened, I put my head under the cover and pretended to be sleep. Whatever was coming in my room that time of night would not bother me because it would think I was already dead…at least that's what I believed. Boy was I wrong. The 'IT' wasn't an IT at all but it was my stepdad or my "DAD as we called him. I was not sure why he was in the room but I suspected he was just checking on us so I just continued to pretend I was asleep. I figured he would just peek in on me and then leave back out the room but that is not what happened. I remember him coming in the room and standing by the bed. He gently sat down on the bed and pulled the cover off me slowly. I didn't move a muscle. I didn't know what was going on but at that time, I was too scared to move or say anything, so I just laid there. I had on a nightgown that was already up around my waist from tossing and turning in my sleep. I remember feeling him pull my panties down and he began to touch my private area. His fingers felt huge and each time he inserted them inside me, it hurt more & more. Each time he kissed my undeveloped breast, I felt sick to my stomach. I wanted to scream, cry, push him away and ask him why he was doing this to me…but instead I didn't move, I didn't say a word. It seemed as if the room was spinning in a vicious circle and I was in the middle of it. I was scared, mad, and so very confused and at that time truly wished mom had let me go with her to the hotel. The whole ordeal lasted maybe five minutes but to me, it seemed as though it lasted forever.

I always heard about things like this happening to little girls in white families, not black families and definitely not MY family and definitely not ME. From the different movies I saw, the families were always white and it never ended up good. I was only a child and didn't know what having a relationship with God was about, but I remember saying to myself, "Lord, why me?"

This was my dad... even though he and mom fought often and even though he called her ugly names and even though he made her cry a lot, this was my dad. Why? Why would he do something like this to me? What did I do to deserve this? Why was he hurting me? What did this mean? At that age I didn't know anything but to lay there and accept what he was doing to me. Kind of the way mom accepted him hitting her and calling her nasty names. And that's what I did as he put his huge fingers inside me and moved them back and forth real slow, I just laid there and accepted it.

I can still feel his enormous hands rubbing on my chest area, rubbing my thighs and my stomach. He never said anything to me and I never saw his face but I could smell him. Not that he smelled bad, but every little girl knows the smell of her daddy. When he was finished he pulled my panties back up, pulled the cover back over me and walked out the room. No words spoken. He walked out as if he had just walked in to check on his precious sleeping daughter. But she, I, wasn't sleeping at all and if that's how a daddy checks on his precious daughter, then I didn't want to be that either. Little did I know, this was just the beginning and there would be many nights of me asking, "Lord, why me?"

The next day nothing was spoken of what happened. He carried on as if everything was normal and although I didn't feel normal, I know what he did to me wasn't normal, I carried on as if everything was normal too. Mom had come back home and everything seemed to be back to its normal state. I wanted to run to her and tell her everything that happened but I didn't. It wasn't until a couple days after the incident that he mentioned what happened. I remember him driving me home from school and him telling me not to tell anyone about what happened. It was strange because he was telling me the same things them white daddy's told their daughters on the movies. He said it was our little secret only and did I understand that I could not tell anyone about it. All I could say was, "Yes Sir" to him but to myself, I was calling myself stupid and dumb just like I heard my mama call the little white girls on the movies. In my mind, I was stupid and dumb. I mean why not? If my mother called them white girls that when those things happened to them and they didn't tell anyone, then I had to be the same because I just said the same things them white girls always said and I knew I wasn't going to tell anyone. So if mom called them stupid, then they must be because we never questioned mom, so in my young mind, that automatically meant, I was stupid too. I simply decided that maybe it was a mistake and would never happen again. I would forget about it and just think about our upcoming move to England.

Well the touching didn't happen again until we were in England. I don't remember the exact date and times while we were in England but I do remember it happening on many many occasions. There are however several occasions that stick out like a sore thumb. Like the many times he would take me from my bed and fondle me on the downstairs couch. This happened, if not every night, at least four to five times a week and the routine was always the same. I would be sleeping in my room with the door closed. He would come into my room, pick me up out my bed and carry me downstairs to the living room and lay me on the couch. I was always awake by the time he got to the bottom of the stairs but I don't think he ever knew it because I pretended to be asleep. Pretending to be asleep became my mental escape so to speak. It was my way of disassociating myself mentally & emotionally with what was actually happening. After he laid me on the couch, he would pull my nightgown up & my panties down and began to fondle my private and my chest area. The way he fondled me was routine as well.

He always began by putting his fingers inside my private, and then he would take a deep breath. Kind of like a sigh of relief of some sort. He then began moving his fingers back & forth. His fingers were huge & this hurt quite a bit, but over time I had learned to suppress the physical pain. I just continued to lie still as if I were asleep. While his fingers were inside me, tearing up the innocence I once had, his other hand would be rubbing my chest area and sometimes I could feel his mouth on my chest. He would be breathing hard & heavy and I would cringe on the inside because of the cigarette stench on his breath. Oftentimes as I lay on the couch, I would pray for someone, anyone to come downstairs and catch him. But it never happened and so the couch abuse, as I call it, continued for some time. It left a very bad impression on me and to this day, I prefer sitting on the floor. There was also the time that I became sick at school and had to call my mother at work. I explained to her I was sick and wanted to go home and she told me that my stepfather would pick me up and take me home. That was the worst thing she could have said at that time and it made me want to just stay at school and suffer but, I couldn't. I was really sick so instead I had to go home and suffer…physically, mentally, and emotionally. Needless to say my stepfather came and picked me up and took me home. When he came into the office at school, I couldn't even look at him. I already knew what was in store for me and reluctantly, I had to leave school. When I got home, I went right upstairs to my room to lie down and wait. It was not long before I heard him calling my name. He was in him and my mother's bedroom, sitting on the bed with this smirk on his face. A smirk that told me he was about to violate me and this time, he didn't have to sneak and do it because we were the only ones at home. I stood by the door, scared and sick. Scared because now that no one was home, I didn't know how long he would fondle me or if he would try to do more to me. I remember him telling me that he needed me to help him make up their bed. I went in the room and stood on my mother's side of the bed and began to pull the sheets up but before I could pull them all the way up he instructed me to get undressed and get in the bed with him. I stood there for a second, thinking I could run downstairs and out the house, but where would I go? Realizing I had nowhere to run to, I reluctantly did as I was told. I accepted that my dad was about to hurt me and I turned my back to him and slowly got undressed. I recall praying that my mom would come home or his job would call and tell him he had to come back to work. I prayed for anything to happen so that I would not have to go through this again, but nothing happened and as I crawled into my parent's bed I was thinking. "Lord, why me?" all over again. As I lay in my parent's bed naked, cold, & feeling dirty, I felt his hands on my body, touching my private parts. As he started in with his routine, I remember going completely numb. I felt that playing dead was the only way for me to get through this. But no matter how dead I pretended to be, I could still feel him. I could feel his hot mouth on my undeveloped chest and his huge fingers in my immature vagina. I also remember him grabbing my hand and putting it on his penis. To me, a small child, it felt huge, hard, and disgusting. I had no idea what to do, so I just laid there, holding his penis in my hand, crying on the inside and screaming the word "STOP" in my head but accepting what he was doing. And he, being an experienced adult, knew everything to do to please himself at the expense of my emotional and mental wellbeing. This entire ordeal lasted for about 20 minutes and when he was finished with me, he got dressed, told me he was going back to work, instructed me to make up the bed and he left. There was no question of if I was alright or anything to show me that he may have been sorry for what he was doing to me. At such a young age I felt like how I thought a whore must feel. I felt dirty and disgusting and I felt something else that at that time I didn't know what it was but now, as an adult, I know it to have been hate. I felt hate inside for this man that I called dad and I felt hate for myself for accepting it.

The sexual abuse went on for many more months while in England. He never changed up his method of 'attack'. He would always come into my room at night, bring me downstairs, and fondle me and he never seemed to get caught in the act. But he eventually did get caught (not in the act but of the act) and the evening I told my mom what was happening to me will forever be stained in my brain.

At the beginning of this story, I was speaking about how I grew up believing that sexual abuse only happened to white little girls and white families. I never saw a movie where it happened to a black little girl and I never heard anyone speak of it happening to a black little girl. Well the night I told my mom what was happening to me we were all sitting in the family room watching a movie. My two brothers, my mother, my stepfather, and I just happened to be watching a movie about a little white girl being sexually abused by her father. My mother was sitting on the couch, I was sitting in front of her on the floor and my stepfather was sitting on the floor but kind of off to the side. I don't recall where my brothers were sitting. I remember during the movie, I absent mindedly started kicking my stepfather's foot. To this day, I have no idea why I was kicking his foot, but I was. He told me to stop and I did for a few minutes, then I would start kicking it again. I remember him telling me to stop again and then a commercial came on the TV. I remember my mother getting up and going into the kitchen. She called me into the kitchen shortly after and asked me why I kept kicking my stepfather's foot. I told her I did not know and truthfully, I did not know why I was kicking him. I remember her leaning against the kitchen counter, looking at me and then she asked me what was going on. Somehow, she knew something was not right. I guess it was her mother's intuition. She assured me that I could talk to her no matter what it was. It was at that moment that I believed all the hurt (physical and emotional) I had endured would stop if I told mom what was going on. I remember thinking to myself, "This is your chance, tell her now." I felt as if I would be saved and finally protected from this animal. I know I needed to tell her, but I was unsure on how she would react. I stared at the floor and before I knew it, I blurted out that he was touching me. She gasped a little but remained quiet for a few seconds. Although I felt like I did the right thing by telling, I didn't get the reaction from her that I expected. She didn't hug me, didn't tell me everything would be ok, didn't cry or yell or even scream. All she did was tell me that she would not tell him that I told her and told me to go back in the front room and watch TV. I honestly don't remember what happened the remaining of the night. I don't even remember if he came in my room that night. All I knew is that I finally told my mother what was going on and she would handle it. She would protect me and make sure that he never touched me again. I was free & had nothing to worry about ever again.

The next few weeks are like a whirlwind in my head. So much was happening and everything was moving super-fast but there are some key things key things that I will never forget as long as I live. I remember one day mom telling me that from now on I needed to push my bed up against my door at night so that he could not come in. Of course I did as instructed and can only remember one time when he tried to open my door but couldn't. Apparently mom had told my stepdad that I told her what he was doing to me. I don't recall hearing them yelling and fussing about it but I briefly recall him having to leave the house. I also recall one day my mother being very very angry about what was going on. I remember her using the restroom, calling me in where she was and out right asking me how I could let this happen. She was yelling at me over and over making it seem as if all of this was my fault, as if I was the one who touched him in the wrong way, as if I, her daughter, was the bad person. I remember her saying how for months she had been having dreams that he was sleeping with her sister, only to find out it was her daughter. She was angry, very angry and it seemed as if her anger was directed at only me. I didn't understand what was going on, but somehow it all seemed to be my fault. When mom yelled at me, I didn't defend myself. I didn't say anything. I just stood there and accepted the blame. My two brothers didn't say much to me about what was going on and I had no real friends to confide in, so I felt very alone. I felt as if I had no one to turn to and talk to about what was happening around me during this time. Mom was angry every single day and it seemed as if she distanced herself from me. I suddenly found myself asking, "Lord, why me?" all the time. I also found myself hating that I said anything and hating him even more for making me hate myself. And to be honest, I wanted to hate mom too because she blamed me.

Like I said earlier, the weeks after I told mom what was happening went by real fast. My stepdad was removed from the house; it seemed as if everyone was walking on egg shells. I do recall meeting a lawyer a time or two. To this day I can't remember what I was told by the lawyer but before I knew it, it was time for us to go to court. The days leading up to court were full of anger, hate, yelling and withdrawal. I had never felt so alone…but this was just the beginning. Before I knew it, it was the day of court and I vividly remember sitting in a small room with this white man, the lawyer, and my mother. I do recall the lawyer asking me if I was ok and telling me that all I had to do was be honest when I was talking to the judge. Mom was unusually quiet as he spoke to me. Although she wasn't yelling and blaming me, I could see on her face that she did not want to be there. But no one wanted to be someplace else more than me. Being a little girl, I didn't know what to expect in court. I was not sure what I was really supposed to say or do. I just remember thinking over and over, Lord, why me? Why is all this happening to me? As I sat in the little room with my head down praying for this to be over, I recall hearing mom ask the lawyer if she could talk to me alone before we go into the court room. I was praying he would say no, but knowing mom, it wouldn't matter if he said yes or no, she was going to have her way. My mother was not a woman to be played with. She was strict and stern and when she spoke, you listened. If she told you to do something, you did it with no questions asked. I guess she was that way because of her years in the military. Anyway when the lawyer left it felt as if the temperature in the room grew cold or maybe it was just my fear creeping up my body. I recall mom turning to me and telling me something that will forever change my relationship with her and how I thought of her. What she said, would change my life forever. She turned to me and, looked me in my eyes and told me when I walk in the courtroom to give my stepfather a hug, tell him I love him, and when I got on the stand to tell the judge that I made the entire story up about him sexually abusing me. As soon as she got the last word out of her mouth, I felt as if my heart had turned to stone. I remember screaming in my head, "WHY!!!" Why would the woman who was supposed to protect me tell me to do such a thing? Why was she not protecting me? Why was she protecting him? I had so many questions and thoughts running through my head and I looked at her but not really seeing her. I didn't try to reason with her about why this felt wrong. I didn't cry my eyes out telling her no, I didn't want to do that. I simply looked at her and said, "Yes ma'am." And as if on cue, the lawyer knocked at the door, peeked his head in, looked at mom, smiled at me and said, "It's time." It was a long slow walk to the courtroom door and when I walked in all eyes were on me. I honestly don't remember thinking or feeling anything at that time. I walked slowly down the short aisle to where he was sitting. I was shaking from both fear & anger. I walked up to him, gave him a hug, told him I loved him and walked to the front of the courtroom and sat next to the judge. I don't know what the judge said to me or asked me. I don't know if any lawyer spoke to me or not. I don't recall if the courtroom was full or empty that day. All I remember is telling the judge that I made the entire story up. I didn't cry and I didn't look at anyone. I don't know how he responded or how anyone else responded but I do remember after all that, one day, my stepfather came back home.

 When he came back home, it seemed as if everything that had happened had been swept under the rug. No one spoke about it at all. It was as if it never happened or had been erased from everyone's memory but mine. Everyone carried on their normal daily routine, including me, but on the inside I was a mess. I started having nightmares about the abuse. Some nights I couldn't sleep and other nights I wouldn't allow myself to sleep. From time to time I found myself in this state of immobility. I would be lying in my bed, wide awake, able to hear and see but unable to speak and move. My only way of getting out of this trance in a sense was for me to literally jump out of it. Every time it happened, I would be in my room alone, with the bed pushed up against the door. So if I had needed help, no one was able to help me. I do remember asking my grandmother about this one day over the phone, I believe, and she told me it was a witch riding my back. She didn't go into detail about it and I didn't ask any more questions about it. I never understand why a witch would ride my back. Was it because I was a bad person or because I was evil in some way? Maybe that was also why my dad abused me and why my mom believed him. Either way, I associated witches with evil and I began to think maybe I was evil as well. Shortly after he came back home, we got word that his mother was dying and we were moving back to the states. Although I don't recall very much about what happened during that time other than the packing and everyone moving around real fast, I do remember never ever wanting to come back to England as long as I live.

THE EYES: Once we came back to the states, I remember sitting in some house that was very poorly lit. The house was filled with people I didn't know and they were walking around whispering and sharing quiet tears. My stepfather's mother has dies and all the people in the house were her family and friends. The house wasn't very big at all and every time someone walked past me, I had to dodge their feet so mine wouldn't get stepped on. When I wasn't trying to save my toes from the many treacherous heels, I was dodging eye contact with everyone who seemed to be looking my way. It could have been my imagination, but I believed they were all staring at me, talking amongst themselves about how I told my mom my stepfather was touching me. The more they stared the angrier I got. It's like I could hear them saying I made the story up. But I didn't and I wanted so bad to scream at the top of my lungs, "He did touch me!! He did!!" I mean these people didn't know me. My brothers and I didn't have a normal grandchild/grandparent relationship with his mother. To this day, I don't even know her name. So how dare his family stare at me (as I truly believed them to be doing) as if I did something wrong. The longer I sat on the couch trying to avoid eye contact, the angrier I became until eventually I realized I had tears streaming down my face. Someone came up and handed me a tissue and told me that grandma was in a better place now. I just looked at the floor because although I was in her house, I felt nothing for her loss of life. I didn't know if I was supposed to or not, so I just got up and went outside to play. I needed to get away from the eyes before I exploded.

THE ARSONIST: I was excited to be going to Ft. Lauderdale to visit my real father. I don't actually remember when the last time was that I saw him, so having this opportunity was the highlight of my life. My real father and my mom divorced when I was too young to remember. He was a short quiet man with the warmest eyes and softest smile I had ever seen. Although he wasn't in me and my oldest brother's life much, I loved him dearly and being able to go visit him always made me the happiest. I remember my mom telling us that we would be in Ft. Lauderdale for a few days so we needed to make sure we packed enough clothes. No one was going except my mom, my two brothers and me. From my understanding, my stepfather had to work and my uncle (my mom's brother) who was visiting us from Germany would also be staying behind. The trip was long and if I remember correctly we got there late at night. I recall being in a hotel and speaking briefly with my real father over the phone before getting ready for bed. The plan was for us to attend church with him the following day. I remember being so excited that it was hard for me to go to sleep. Little did I know, I would not get to see my father on Sunday, April 17, 1988. It would be a day forever embedded in my mind. I remember waking up to the phone ringing. Mom answered it and all I heard her say was, "A fire!" I had no idea what she was talking about. Where was a fire? Who was calling us so early to talk about a fire? I didn't realize the urgency in her voice as being what it was; I just knew something about a fire. Mom woke up my oldest brother and also called my real father. The one thing that I replayed in my mind was when my mom told my father that he would not be able to see us because we had to rush back home. Instantly, my heart dropped out my body and rolled away. I was devastated. At that point I didn't care about a fire or the panicked look my mom had on her face. I just wanted to see my daddy. I don't remember the drive back home or even leaving the hotel for that matter. What I do remember is eventually seeing the home that we used to live in for the first time. I remember returning to school, walking into my classroom late and the entire class staring at me and whispering. I was embarrassed, sad, and confused all at the same time. After school one particular day, I rode the school bus home with my friend. After we got off the bus, we walked to what was once a beautiful, two-story, four-bedroom home now represented by four brick walls covered in soot and ash. All I remember seeing left of our personal items was a refrigerator. I even remember another friend of mine making a joke about the burned items that used to be in the refrigerator. I didn't cry or yell, I simply looked at what was left of our belongings...absolutely nothing. I remember feeling as if everything was a horrible nightmare and I had no idea what was going on. I was 10 years old when this happened and as a child when your house burns down and you realize you have nothing, you hope and pray that you are having a horrible nightmare. As time went on, I remember hearing my mother and stepfather talking about how my uncle got burned in the fire. Although he was blessed to be alive, he did suffer very bad burns over his entire body. I also remember them saying something about the fire being arson and how my stepfather was being accused of burning the house down with my uncle. I remember him having to go to court and them winning the case. I don't recall actually being in the courtroom, so I'm sure most of what I remember about the arson was due to the conversations I overheard at home, at school, and amongst my friends. I recall seeing something in the newspaper about the suspected arson and feeling really strange about it all.

Recently as I was thinking about the arson at work, I had the idea to search for the newspaper clippings. I honestly didn't think I would find them but I did. A young gentleman at the public library system in Tampa was able to locate the articles as written in the Tampa Tribune & St.

Petersburg Times. One of the articles had a picture of the house after the fire. As I sat and stared at the picture I became overwhelmed with emotion and then I remembered something that was told to me in my early 20's. Something I'll never forget as long as I live… something that sent chills down my spine and immediately made me sick just thinking of it. As I got up from my desk at work and rushed to the restroom, all I could ask myself was why. No child can prepare themselves to receive the news I received about this fire and the arsonist and no child should have to.

A NORMAL LIFE AGAIN: Sometime after the house had burned down, my brothers and I found ourselves living with my grandmother. I don't recall the exact reasoning as to why we were staying with her, but I recall being told that we would be there until my mom and stepdad got the house situated. I was ok with the choice that was made because as long as I was in Georgia and my stepdad was in Florida, I didn't have to worry about him touching me. My grandmother is a strong woman whom I love deeply and living with her was heaven for me. I had the opportunity to be around all my cousins and we had a blast with one another. We were all close in age so we got along pretty good. Mommy, as we called my grandmother, lived in a very small country town in Georgia and was well known throughout the town as well as some neighboring towns. She is a devout Christian and had us in church several times a week. Mommy was the one who introduced God into my life and it was while living with her that I got baptized for the first time. The name of our church was Bethel Primitive Baptist Church and it was definitely 'primitive' in my young eyes. The Pastor was much older and every 1st Sunday in addition to communion we also had a feet washing ceremony. This is where the younger generation had to wash the feet of the older generation. This was in remembrance of when Mary washed Jesus' feet in the bible. I didn't understand why we did this, but we children had no choice in the matter as long as Mommy was present. It was while living with my grandmother that I decided to give my life to Christ. The day I got baptized was special for me. In my mind and my heart, it was the day that I accepted God in my life and I knew that once I came out the water it would mean I would be cleansed...at least that's what I was told. I remember wearing a white robe and standing in the pool at the front of the church. The Pastor was asking me some questions and every time he asked me something I looked over at Mommy who was nodding her head in approval. As long as she was giving her approval, then I knew what I was about to do was the right thing. Also just the Sunday before, my older brother had gotten baptized. I remember thinking that if he did it, then I know I needed to do it as well. As my mind was drifting off, wondering what it would be like to be cleansed in my soul, I remember being dunked under water with no warning and immediately being brought back up. The baptism took less than three minutes and before I knew it I was being guided out the pool to the back of the church. I heard people clapping and praising God. Something in me told me God was pleased with me and so, I was pleased with myself. I remember thinking to myself, "I did it! I was baptized and cleansed!" I was so proud of myself and expected Mommy to be proud of me too but as soon as I got to the back of the church I recall Mommy fussing at me because my bra was not clean. She was saying how people could see my dirty bra through the white gown and how embarrassed she was. I laugh now because I was a kid and didn't realize that having a clean bra was that important to where Mommy would be furious with me on the day that my soul was cleansed. But apparently, it was because her disappointment in me that day was very evident. So what I thought should have been a great day, turned into an ok day. One thing about Mommy, she did not like being embarrassed in public. Mommy was also very no nonsense when it came to church and God and as most southern black grandmothers in that time, she forbid us to act up in church. I can laugh now, but during the time I lived with her, the consequences of acting up in church were brutal as Mommy did not believe in sparing the rod, or the switch, or the water hose pipe. I recall so many times that she beat all of us just because one of us acted up. But regardless of the whoopings we received, living in the country was great. I will never forget the stillness at night. Besides the crickets chirping, you heard absolutely nothing. I remember the times we had to work in the fields and pick butterbeans or we had to pick pecans from my grandmother's pecan trees. It was hot and my cousins and I often talked about feeling like Hebrew Slaves working for Master as we bent over in the fields trying to hurry and fill our buckets. I remember during the winter months Mommy would make early morning fires and we would get dressed in front of the fireplace. Plenty times I would wake up and just sit in front of the fireplace and stare at the fire often wondering how hot hell was. I would sit for long periods of time until my thoughts were interrupted by someone standing in front of me blocking my heat. I loved everything about country living. Even going to the chicken coup to get the eggs and hanging the laundry on the line outside. But most of all, I loved the great soul food my grandmother prepared daily for us to eat. She truly cooked her food with love. Although I have lived overseas and in the big city, I am a true country girl to heart and that's something I will forever be.

While staying with Mommy, I was in the 6th grade and attended Willow Hill School. I didn't know a lot of the children at the school but I became semi popular pretty fast. See, although I was not allowed to have a boyfriend, I did what most young girls do; I snuck and had one anyway. He was the most popular boy in school. He was tall and dark skinned and very country and no one could tell me I wasn't in love. His name was Craig. Craig was very sweet and made me laugh all the time. He had the prettiest smile and his eyes reminded me of my real father. He was my boyfriend the entire school year so needless to say, the school year was a great one. I remember after the school year had ended and we were just getting into our summer routines Mommy told my brothers and me that my mom and stepfather would be coming to pick us up and take us back to Florida. I instantly went into panic mode. All I could think about was my stepfather touching again. As the thoughts and fears of him touching me flooded my brain, I told myself there was no way; I was going back to Florida. I began to formulate a plan in my head so that I did not have to. As my cousin and I lay in our room talking instead of sleeping as Mommy instructed us to do, I decided to share my plan with her. She and I were only a year apart and very close. We shared all our secrets with one other and I knew that I could trust her to keep what I was about to tell her to herself as well as help me carry it out. So as we lay in the bed, I told her my plan and made her swear not to say anything to anyone. She agreed and it was set. The next morning, I was going to run away. In my mind, that was the only way I would be able to get away from the abuse…from him. After I told her my plans and we giggled some more, we finally fell off to sleep. The next morning, before day, while everyone was still asleep, I woke up, dressed, and slipped out the bedroom window. My cousin woke up and told me not to go. She was scared and so was I, but my mind was made up. To me running away was the right thing to do and so, I walked…and walked…and walked for about a mile and a half. Running away was as far as I had planned and it dawned on me that I had not decided where I would run to or what I would eat. But I refused to turn around, I refused to be scared, I refused to be hurt again. As I was walking, I came upon a small store with a payphone. I knew I couldn't call Mommy because she would just come get me, take me back home, and probably whoop my behind with two switches twisted together. So instead, I called Craig. I told him I had run away from home and why and he agreed to meet me at the high school. Within about 20 minutes, I saw him walking towards me. I knew he wouldn't let me down, he loved me and when someone loves you, they don't let you down. They don't turn their backs on you in your time of need. When he approached me, we hugged, he grabbed my hand and we began to walk. I had never been to Craig's house so I had no idea where he was taking me, but I trusted him. We were definitely the blind leading the blind. As we were walking, we didn't talk much. My mind was racing because I knew by now Mommy had discovered that I was not at the house. I was thinking what was she saying, was she worried, mad, sad?? Had my cousin told on me or did she keep her promise? My mind was everywhere and so preoccupied with what if's that I never heard the car pull up behind us until the driver honked the horn. I turned around and to my surprise and fear, I saw Mommy. In the car with her were my aunt, my oldest brother, and my cousin. Mommy pulled up beside us and asked me what I was doing. I had nothing to say and held my head down. I was caught. She asked Craig who he was and told him who she was and then she told me to get in the car. I looked at Craig, said goodbye and got in the backseat with my brother and cousin. Mommy drove off and home we went. I didn't get a whooping like I expected to. My aunt was telling me how worried they were and that I can never do that again. I honestly don't remember if anyone asked me why I ran away and if they did, I'm almost sure I didn't go into detail about the abuse. I'm sure I just said that I ran away because I didn't want go to Florida. Now that I think of it, the abuse never came up the entire time I lived with mommy that school year. A few weeks later, we were living back home with my mom and stepdad in Tampa. Lord, Why Me???

    *7th **GRADE**:* There are three main events that I really remember about the 7th grade. Three events that will always make me remember my 7th grade school year. One event being that the sexual abuse started back up. We were living in some apartments. It was a 3 bedroom apartment and we lived downstairs. With mom being in the military, there were times she had to leave for periods of time either for schooling or training. I remember one time mom had to go to some schooling for her job and my stepdad stayed home and watched my two brothers and me. With mom gone, he made sure to violate me often. One particular night that sticks out in my head the most would be the one night I was watching television. My brothers were asleep but I wanted to see if I could stay up all night without falling asleep. I remember I was lying on the couch on my stomach and I had my bedspread covering me. I was watching cartoons and trying so hard not to fall asleep. My eyes had become heavy and just as I was about to drift off to sleep, he came and sat down on the couch by my feet. I remember him putting his hand under the cover, under my night gown and inside my panties. I squirmed a little hoping he would leave me alone but he didn't. Sleep or not, he was going to do what he wanted at the expense of my emotional and mental well being. And he did just that. He moved my panties to the side and began to rub on my private. I squirmed some more, and in my squirming as soon as he found the opening to my young vagina, he stuck his fingers in and began to finger me. His hands were huge and it hurt badly but I didn't cry. Something deep inside me told me to just lay there and I did. I guess that is what my body was used to doing so it just reverted to what it knew. I lay on that couch as he forced his fingers in and out of me. I laid there and accepted the hurt, the pain, the torture. I laid there and after a few minutes I realized that I had a taste of blood in my mouth. I had been biting my tongue and didn't even know it. I didn't even feel the pain of my teeth sinking down into my flesh. That was my first taste of hate. I hated this man who violated me at his will. I hated that I had to call him dad. I hated that I had to be in the same house with him every single day. I hated his smell, his touch, his crooked smile. I hated him and I hated myself. As I lay on that couch I hated myself for not going to bed when my brothers did. How could I have been so stupid? I had so many thoughts running through my head and I wished that my brothers would wake up and catch him. Why did they sleep so hard? As I was tearing myself up verbally in my mind, he was tearing me up mentally, tearing me down emotionally, and tearing me apart physically. After what seemed like hours, he stopped. He removed his hands from what had now become his vagina and told me to get up and go to bed. He didn't even bother moving my panties back in place. Before I could move, he got up and left the room. It was not until he was out of the room that I got up from the couch, swallowed the bloody spit that had gathered in my mouth, and wobbled to my bedroom. I laid on my bed and cried silent tears. Why was this happening to me? Tears from the mental pain as well as the physical soaked my pillow. As I thought back to England and when the abuse began, I cried deep heart wrenching cries. This pain was too familiar to me and I hated it.

CLOSET FIRE: Another incident I recall would be when my younger brother set the closet on fire. Although this could have turned out very very bad it is now quite funny to me. It was around Fourth of July. We were still in the same apartments and my mom and stepdad had bought us some sparklers. My oldest brother, mom, and stepdad were in the front part of the apartment when all of a sudden we smelled smoke. We didn't know where it was coming from at first but eventually realized it was coming from my brother's room. I remember either my mother or my stepfather running in the room and my younger brother was sitting on the floor with his back against the closet door and the room was quickly filling up with smoke. When the closet door was opened all you could see were flames shooting everywhere. We had to rush out the house and our neighbors called 911. My brother had been playing with a sparkler in the closet and some of the embers had dropped on some clothes hanging up. By the time the fire trucks arrived, all of my oldest brother's clothes were burned as well as his shoes and there was a crowd of people standing outside our apartment building. I will never ever forget that day. My younger brother got a good talking to by the fire fighters and that was the end of my mom and stepdad buying fireworks.

TOO OLD TO DATE: This last incident has to do with me and a young man. This young man was not a student at my school, as a matter of fact he was old enough to be out of high school but with his boyish looks, he could pass for a teen. I met him one day during P.E. My class was outside and there was a sitting area close to the school. The students as well as the neighborhood people always sat in this sitting area. Well this particular day while outside this young man was sitting in this area and he began to talk to me. I honestly don't remember his name but he gave me his phone number. I recall a few times during the weeks he would be hanging around this sitting area and when ever my class went outside, I would talk to him. The teachers never noticed and if they did, they never said anything. Maybe because there was more than one class outside the teachers thought he was a student in another class. Anyway, this young man and I talked all the time. I liked him & he liked me. One day I ended up skipping school to be with him. I remember we just spent the day walking around his neighborhood, holding hands, kissing, laughing and being silly. He stayed with his grandmother and this particular day he took me to his house. When we got there we sat around the house, ate something, and went to his room. I was scared because I had never been with a boy sexually. I mean I knew what it felt like to be touched but not to be touched willingly. As we lay on his bed kissing and talking I thought something was going to happen. I thought he was going to try and have sex with me…but he didn't. He told me that although he wanted to, he refused to touch me in any type of sexual way because I was so much younger than him and he was scared to go to jail. We ended up only staying there for about 30 minutes then he took me back to school just in time for me to catch the school bus home. As we walked up to the school, he gave me a hug and I got on my bus to go home. We saw one another a few more times at the school but I never skipped school with him again. Eventually I started liking another boy who was a student at my school. As I write this all out, I'm thinking how naïve and stupid I was to have skipped school with some man that I didn't know well enough. He could have raped or killed me and no one would have known what happened. That was one of the dumbest things I did. I oftentimes wonder, had he killed me, would my mom have missed me? Would my brothers have cried? Would my stepfather have been sorry for abusing me?

A child is a child until their innocence is torn away from them.

Part 2: A Raging War on the Inside.

After the 7th grade, the sexual abuse didn't happen again until I was in the 9th grade. I think this is because in the 8th grade my mother allowed me to have my first real boyfriend. Well at least the one she actually knew about. I won't mention his name but he would later become my 2nd husband. My 8th grade year was great!! I was dating a boy who I had grown to love and every chance our parents allowed us, we spent it together. We went to the movies, school dances, and visited each other's homes several times. He and I talked on the phone every single day for hours at a time. As a matter of fact, he would be the one I almost lost my virginity to. My 8th grade year was great in my eyes not just because my stepfather didn't touch me but because I was in love. At the end of 8th grade, my boyfriend informed me that his father was retiring from the military and they would be moving to Atlanta, GA. I was devastated. That was the first time that my heart had been broken. I remember crying when he moved away. When he got to Atlanta, he and I spoke almost every day until we were instructed by our parents that the phone bills were getting to high and we had to resort to writing letters. After a few months, we stopped talking altogether and soon after that the abuse started up again. My 9th grade year is when shit started to get crazy for me and the raging war in my mind began.

BESTFRIENDS: Sometime during my 8th grade school year we moved to another part of town and my 9th grade year I had to change schools. My mother started taking me to a friend's house every morning so that I could attend the same school but eventually it got to be too much for her. So in the middle of 9th grade, I was no longer attending Burns Jr. High School which was a majority white preppy school. I was now attending Dowdell Jr. High which was a majority black school and known for its reputation which was not a good one. Admit tingly, I was scared as hell to go to this school. I didn't know anyone at who attended this school and I missed all my friends from Burns terribly. I felt that I would not fit in. I was lonely but not for long. I eventually met a young girl who would later become my very best friend. She lived with her father, sisters and brothers and once she and I met and hit it off, we were inseparable. In a sense I looked at her as the sister I never had. We did everything together, we shared secret crushes with one another, we skipped school together, we laughed and we cried together. She was truly my very best friend. Although mom often told my friend that she loved her like a daughter and that she could talk to her anytime about anything, Mom thought she was to grown acting because she wore makeup and weave. There were times she would come to my house and my mother smiled and grinned in her face but as soon as she left mom had nothing nice to say. It bothered me that mom was like that but there was nothing anyone could say to me that would make me stop being her friend. I truly loved her as my sister.

ALCOHOL WAS HER ESCAPE: Although my mother was in the Air Force, she was what I call a functional alcoholic. She would come home from work and hit the bottle everyday. GIN was her drink of choice and it later became my first drink of choice. There were times when mom would get so drunk that I would be scared for her. I would be scared she would lose her job, but she didn't. She could be extremely drunk one night and get up the next morning ready for work. And unless you were in the house with us, you would never have guessed she drank like she did. As a child, I didn't know what drove her to drink. I did however notice that my stepfather didn't drink but he made sure to keep the house stocked with wine and liquor. I also noticed that when mom drank, there was bound to be an argument or worse…a fight between her and him. I recall one time they were fussing about something only God knows and my stepdad started beating mom. Of course this wasn't the first time, as my brothers and I had witnessed these beating on several occasions. But this particular night, the beating was bad and I was terrified he would kill her. Regardless of the fact that we were standing right there, I remember him punching her and spitting on her. I looked at my older brother pleading with him through my eyes to do something. I knew he was scared…we all were scared. My older brother and I watched in horror as my mom tried to fight him back and my younger brother did what he always did, ran back to his room. I recall at some point my older brother trying to jump in and stop the fighting but my stepfather pushed him out the way. I don't know what was running through my head, but I remember running in the kitchen grabbing a butcher knife and yelling for him to leave my mom alone. He looked at me, square in the eyes and said, "Oh so you want to pull a knife on me?" I didn't say a word back, but I didn't move either. He must have seen the rage in my eyes because he backed away and walked out the house. I don't know what I would have done had he came any closer to me, but I suppose I would have tried to kill him. In an instant, I had become my mother's protector, willing to die for her and even kill for her. I was prepared to stop him from hurting her. I was clearly in a place that a child should never have to be in. I was taking the protective role for her...the role she never took for me. As I am remembering, I want to cry but I can't. Anyway either my older brother or my mother called 911 and the police arrested my stepdad that night. I remember my older brother being so upset and telling my mom that if she went and got him out of jail that time, we were going to go live with mommy and never come back. Sadly, that threat held no weight because some days later, my stepdad had come back home. The fighting between them continued and the abuse was back in full effect. We never went to my grandmother's and mom continued to drink her troubles away. Her drinking was bad…so bad that she would say things to us that left us in tears and turmoil. I remember one day it was just my younger brother, my mom, and I at home. I was in my room taking a nap and my younger brother was crying and banging on my door. I jumped up to see what was going on and he told me that my mom had told him she was going to kill herself and make it look like an accident so we could get the insurance money. I was so furious that I began to cry. I recall yelling and asking her why would she say something like that to her child. She just stood there drunk, with a smirk on her face and said, "Well at least if I die you all will get paid." I just looked at her and shook my head. I could not believe that a mother would purposely say something like that knowing full well it would scare the hell out of her children. It was not until many years later, when I became an adult, that I realized mom drank the way she did because of guilt, depression, and I believe apart of her saw herself as a failure of a mother to my brothers and me. Drinking and willingly going into a drunken stupor almost daily was her way of handling her own pain that I also believe she still carries to this day. The alcohol made it to where she would not have to deal with her pain, but it also drove her to a dark place and locked her in.

ALMOST PENETRATED: Since the start of the sexual abuse, my stepfather had always just touched me or fondled my private areas with his hand. That all changed on the day he almost penetrated me. I was home with my younger brother one day. My mom and stepdad were at work. I'm not sure where my older brother was. He eventually moved out the house so I'm not sure if this incident was before or after him leaving. Anyway, my younger brother and I were at home watching TV when I heard my stepfather's work truck pull up. He was a delivery driver for an alcohol distribution company. (This is how he was able to keep the house stocked with alcohol for my mom.) After he parks his truck and comes in the house, he immediately tells me to clean him and my mom's bathroom and tells my younger brother that he could go outside. My brother puts on his shoes and wastes no time dashing out the door and around the corner to go play. I on the other hand began to feel sick. I knew the reason he sent my brother outside was so that he could abuse me. I go in the bathroom to begin cleaning but before I can even get started he comes in the room and calls me to their bed. Déjà Vu kicks in because I have been in this place before…back in England. As I am standing in front of the bed, he tells me to lie back and I do as I'm told. He kneels down in front of me and pulls my shorts and my panties down and begins to touch my private with his hands. I'm a teenager. I have learned about sex from friends and school. I have pubic hair, my breasts have grown and I had already started my period years earlier. Needless to say, the touching felt different to me this time. As he was touching my private, inserting his finger in and out I just laid on the bed trying to compose myself. This touching was not supposed to make my body feel the way it was feeling. I tried to dismiss the feelings but honestly, I did not know what the hell was happening to me. As I was trying to figure out why my body had deserted my mind's thought of this act being disgusting I heard him unzip his pants. He pulled his pants down and began to rub the head of his penis up and down my vagina. I instantly felt my insides get moist but I had no idea why. I didn't know what my body was doing but it was completely out of control. Before I knew it I reached my hand down between my legs and grabbed his penis and tried to make him stick it inside me. It was obvious that his perverted spirit had jumped from him to me because this was not how I was supposed to react. I remember thinking to myself that the original plan was to lie still as though I were asleep or dead any time he touched me. That's what I had always done so why was I not able to do that now? Even though I was a child and he the adult and even though my right states of mind did not want this man touching me, my body was reacting against my better judgment. When I grabbed him, he moved my hands away, got up abruptly and went into the restroom. I got up and ran to my bedroom, closed and locked the door and burst into tears. I was totally ashamed and disgusted with myself. I was confused as to what had just happened and why I reacted in the way that I did. Although he never penetrated me, I hated myself for many years after this incident. I know now that as a young teenager, my body was reacting to his touch and even though it was not something that I desired…it was not something I could control at that time. My body just reacted. It took many many years for me to understand that and come to terms with myself because for years I felt as though I was egging him on to touch me. I felt that he believed I wanted it or liked it, but that's the furthest from the truth. To this day I believe that had his penis not been so big in comparison to my teenage vagina, he would have had sex with me that day.

RAPED: Being the new kid in school is never easy but I made out ok at Dowdell. I think a lot of it had to do with my best friend. She was very popular in school and I think it helped my little social life. After being at the school for a little while, I met this young boy at school. Although he was in the 9th grade, he seemed to be older. He wasn't in school much but once I found out he liked me, that didn't bother me. On the days he did come to school we would walk home together. He lived on the street in back of my house so we were going the same way. We spent our nights talking on the phone and just being teenagers. One evening as we were talking on the phone he asked if he could come over. I told him my mother and my 2 brothers were home. My stepfather had not come home from work yet. He told me he just wanted to talk, nothing else. I knew mom had been drinking and was passed out on the couch and my brothers were asleep so I agreed. The plan was for me to let him through my bedroom window, we would just talk, and he would leave out the way he came in. As soon as I agreed, I got an uneasy feeling and called him back and told him I had changed my mind. I was scared. He got upset and told me that he was coming anyway and if I didn't open the patio door he would cut the screen.

Believing him and not wanting to get in trouble if he did cut the screen door, I cut the alarm wire to my window so the alarm would not sound off, opened my window, crawled out and unlocked the patio door. I then locked my bedroom door and sat on the bed waiting for him to knock on my window. After about ten minutes he knocked. As I sat on the bed contemplating on if I should let him in, I realized I was shaking. I was scared of getting caught and excited to see him all at the same time. I allowed my excitement to overrule my fear and I opened my window and he crawled in. We sat on the bed and talked for a little while. We were everyday teenagers, whispering and giggling trying not to get caught. As we were talking, he leaned over and kissed me. Next thing I knew he was on top of me and I could feel his penis growing harder and harder under his pants. I whispered to him to stop, but he didn't. He held me down, pulled my panties down and forced his penis deep inside me. I winced in pain. It was so much pain and it seemed as though it ricocheted through my bones. I begged him to stop, but he would not. He kept thrusting himself inside my freshly broken vagina and eventually I stopped talking and just laid there with tears running down my face as he raped me. I thought back to the times my stepdad abused me and I just laid there and played dead. I just wanted him to finish before anyone woke up. About 2 minutes after he started, he stopped. He got up, pulled his pants up, called me a little scared girl, and hopped out my window walking away into the night. I put my hands between my legs and when I looked at my hand, there was blood. I cried. I managed to get up & hop out the window to lock the patio door back. After I came back inside, I stripped the sheets off my bed and threw them in the back of my closet. I had done something terribly wrong and I needed to hide the evidence. My vagina was on fire but I wobbled to the bathroom and cleaned myself up. Once I got back to my room, I mean as soon as I shut the door, mom woke up. I heard her shuffling to her bed bumping into the walls every few steps. She was to drunk to realize that her baby girl had just been violated…again. I put on new bed sheets but slept on the floor that night. My bed had become a foreign object to me. The next morning we all woke up doing our normal morning routines. I remember mom walking by and stopping in front of my room. I looked up and noticed she was looking at the alarm pad. There was a red light next to bedroom 3. Bedroom 3 was my room. She asked me if I knew why the light was on and I denied knowing anything. I was scared and closed my door. Within about 10 minutes she came bursting into my room asking about some footprints leading to my window. I played dumb. Earlier that morning while mom was in the shower and I was in my room dressing, I noticed my stepdad was standing outside my window peeping on me. He did this often when he felt he could get away with it so I thought to myself that maybe the footprints were his. But I still denied knowing anything. Mom came back in the room and looked up at my window and noticed the wire was cut. She called my stepdad in the room and he confirmed what she already knew, the wires had been cut with a razor. By this time, there was no denying anything. I confessed to letting the boy in the house and told my mom that he forced me to have sex. I began to cry, telling her that he raped me. Although I knew I was wrong for my part, I didn't believe I deserved to be raped. My mother on the other hand had a different way of thinking. Instead of her consoling me about the rape, she began to call me all kind of names. I was a bitch, a slut, and a whore twenty times over. I deserved what happened to me .That morning I was everything except a child of God who made the wrong decision and was sexually violated. She called me so many bad names. After making me feel worse than I already did, after she instructed me not to go to school and for my older brother to stay home with me, and she and my stepfather left for work. After her and my stepdad left, I remember my older brother asking me why I did what I did. I didn't have an answer and I knew he was mad at me. I remember thinking how his little sister had turned into a mess. I stayed in my room the remainder of the day and cried and cried. I told myself over and over that I would be better off dead. I did not believe that I deserved to live amongst the "good" because I was so "horrible". That is when I decided to end my life. I don't recall my brother coming in to check on me as I cried my heart out. After a few hours, I was totally convinced that I deserved to die. Everyone hated me but not as much as I hated myself. I needed to die. I went into the bathroom and got the bottle of Tylenol out the medicine cabinet. I came back into my room, laid on the floor by the foot of the bed and slowly began to swallow one pill after another. I don't remember how many I took, and I didn't care. I just wanted to die and be forgotten. Before I knew it, I had drifted off to sleep or either I was unconscious. The next thing I remembered was waking up to my mother shouting my name.

When I had come too, she almost looked disappointed, at least to me. She could not have been more disappointed than I was to realize that I was still alive. Why had I not died? Why was God allowing me to live? I remember mom telling me to get up so we could go to the hospital. I also remember there being no type of comforting from her. She did not even look as though she was worried for me. When I looked in her eyes, all I saw was disgust. We went to the hospital and according to the doctor, had I taken a few more pills, I would have had to have my stomach pumped. I also remember talking to the police about the rape but refusing to press charges on the boy. This was after my mom and step dad had went to the boys home and spoke with either his mother or grandmother and she informed him that he was involved in another rape case where he left the young girl for dead in some ditch. She too later dropped charges against him. After that whole incident, I later found out the boy was a drug dealer and had gotten arrested for another crime. He was serving time in prison. To this day, I don't know what became of him.

CUTTING WAS MY ESCAPE: After the rape, I began to sink into a depression. I preferred to stay in my room and read or write versus sitting in the living room with the rest of the family. I felt as though I didn't belong in that family and often times I told myself I was adopted and my real parents would come rescue me. Deep down I was hurting and no one seemed to understand or even care. There were times when I would get extremely angry or upset with myself or things that have happened and I just had to release my pain. My way of releasing my pain was by seeing my own blood. My cutting was my way of escaping the reality of my now totally screwed up life. When I felt like things were getting to heavy for me and my mind became cloudy, I would grab my razor and cut on my wrist. The intent was never to kill myself; I just needed to see my blood. I know it may sound crazy, but in my mind seeing my blood helped keep me calm. Mentally I would believe that as my blood oozed out the cuts, my hurt, anger, rage and pain oozed out as well and I would be able to think clearly. To this day the only person in my family who knew I cut myself was my stepdad. He didn't find out because I told him. He found out because one evening as I was sitting on the floor in my bedroom with razor in hand and tears rolling down my face, I noticed a shadow outside my bedroom window. It was him, being a peeping tom again. This particular night I was bold. I knew he could see me even though the blinds were turned down so I took the razor I was holding, stood in front of the window and made several cuts on my left arm. I watched the blood trickle out and instantly felt a relief in my spirit. I looked up and he was still standing there and after a few seconds he walked away. He never said anything to me about it and he never mentioned it to my mom. But then again how could he, he was not going to blow his cover by telling her he was watching me through my bedroom window. That night I learned that if I turn my blinds upward then he couldn't see through them into my bedroom. To this very day the blinds in my home must be turned upwards for my own peace of mind

WE KILLED MY BABY: At the start of the 10th grade, I was pretty much living in a hell hole called home but I tried so hard to front as if I was a happy teen living in a happy house. So many things were happening daily and with each event, I was withdrawing more and more from everyone. For some reason, mom had randomly started checking me again. Sometime after the abuse, she had started this practice of checking me to see if my vagina had been disturbed. She had stopped but oddly started back up in the 10th grade. I guess the whole rape ordeal made her feel some type of way and she thought that checking me daily would alert her to something going on. She would come home from work, change clothes, come into my room and tell me to remove my bottoms and my panties. I then would be instructed to lay on the bed with my legs propped open and she would began to poke, prod, and pull at my womanhood. After she found nothing she would just walk out the room without a word. The few times that she saw some redness, she would go into detective mode and start asking me fifty questions. Why was I redder than I was the day before? Who had I been allowing to touch me? Had I stuck anything down there? And many more accusing and embarrassing questions. She treated me like I was a criminal and not her child. Even if I knew that I was red because her husband had fondled me, I didn't say anything to her about it. As a matter of fact, there were plenty times that the reason was exactly that. I never told anyone this, but the way she treated me during my examination made me feel dirty and I often felt as though I was getting abused all over again. It sickened me to my core. By now, I had lost all confidence in her as my mother. I saw her as just the woman providing for me. I knew her ability to protect me was gone so although the sexual abuse continued, I kept it to myself. She didn't do anything the first time I told her so what was the point in telling her it was still going on, more than likely she still would not do anything about it. That is how I felt.

Because I was so miserable, I started to cut more frequently. I would cut in the mornings before school as well as in the evenings before bed. I always had my cuts covered so no one would find out what I was doing. And even during the hot Florida summer days when I wore long sleeves, no one ever questioned me. The cutting lasted all the way into my first marriage. The last time I cut, I was 21 years old, married, with two children.

Although the cutting helped a little in keeping me calm, some days it just wasn't enough. Some days I needed something to fully numb me inside and out. I needed something that would make me forget the pain I felt every single day. That something was alcohol. Just like my mother, Gin was my drink of choice. I would wake up in the mornings, get dressed for school and as I was in the kitchen, I would fix some orange juice and gin. I always poured it in a sports bottle and made sure to add water to the gin bottle to hide what I had stolen. This became my daily fix and if there was no OJ, I used Kool-Aid, or any kind of juice available. One day I even used milk. I took a drink to school daily. I remember on several occasions sitting in my first period class drunk as hell, not hearing anything nor talking to anyone. I was at a point where I simply did not care if I got caught or not. In my mind, my life was worthless and what ever happened just happened. Amazingly my teachers never knew or at least they never said anything. Bringing alcohol to school only lasted a few months. I realized I was turning into something I didn't want to be, and my mom was starting to notice that her gin tasted different. I would later pick the drinking back up in my adult years.

Sometime during my sophomore year, I met a young high school senior. I don't recall how we met but eventually he and I started dating. He was older than me and he went to a different high school then me, but that didn't stop us from seeing one another every chance we got. We met up at football games, basketball games…wherever. I found myself falling for him hard, so hard that I even began skipping school and classes just to be with him. In a way, I believed we understood one another and loved each other. He was the first guy that I willingly went all the way with sexually. He didn't pressure me or make me feel bad when he first asked and I said no. He told me he would wait until I was ready, and he did. Well, I had always heard that it only takes one time to get pregnant and that's exactly what happened. About a month after we had sex, I missed my period. I was terrified. I immediately told him that I was pregnant and he was excited. A little too excited for me. I had no idea how to tell my mother that I was pregnant and part of me felt that if I told her she would beat the hell out of me. See I never had the "birds & bees" conversation with my mom. We never sat down and talked about birth control, condoms, STDs, or pregnancy. All she ever said was for me not to get pregnant at 16. She didn't even notice any change in my eating habits or sleeping habits, so I felt that I had some time to buy before I told her my secret. The only other person who knew besides my boyfriend was my best friend, but not for long. I remember the day mom found out I was pregnant as if it were yesterday. I had skipped school to hang out with some friends. By the time I got home, my mother's car was in the driveway. I was instantly nervous because she should have been at work still. When

I walked in the house, she waited until I had put my books down before she confronted me about not being in school that day. She said she got a recorded call from the school saying that I was absent. Before I had a chance to answer her, she told me she was going to beat my ass. She went back to her room to get her belt. As soon as she turned away, I grabbed her car keys and ran out the house. I was terrified of what was about to happen and I knew that I was pregnant and I didn't want my baby to get hurt. When I got to the bottom of the driveway mom was standing at the front door, I yelled that I had skipped school and that I was pregnant and I threw her keys in the yard and took off running down the street. The reason I threw her keys was because I did not want her to follow me, and she would have. I don't know what I was thinking or where I was going but I just needed to get away. I was scared, mad at myself for letting this happen, and mad at my mom. I ended up at my best friend's house and together we caught the city bus to her grandmother's house in the projects. I don't recall how long I stayed there but I remember talking to my oldest brother and him telling me that my mom said I could not come back to her house. I was devastated. Here I was a 10th grader, pregnant with no means to care for myself or a baby. I remember lying across a bed, needing to cut, needing to drink, and wanting to die. I had to come to terms with the fact that there was a person growing inside me and I had no idea about what I was going to do? I'm not sure how long I stayed gone, but eventually, I was allowed to come back home. I'm not sure what made her change her mind, but she did. The day I walked back into the house, she and my stepdad were waiting for me with open arms. They had even ordered some Red Lobster for me. Mom was unusually nice and caring and she even seemed excited. I, on the other hand, was scared. This may sound crazy, but I was scared she was going to jump on me and beat me. But she didn't. I ate the food they had bought and within minutes of finishing, I ran to the restroom and brought it all back up. Mom was right there by my side, making sure I was ok. It was odd seeing her in a loving, caring position but I accepted it. I was so used to mom being very stern and hard. The next memory I have of this pregnancy is sitting in an abortion clinic with my mother. She had decided that I was not going to have this baby I was too young. I agree that I was young, but she never asked me how I felt about having an abortion. She never asked if I wanted to keep my baby. She didn't ask me anything, she just made the decision and as usual, I fell in line. The abortion clinic was just a small building, like a doctor's office. There were other people in the office, but I only saw their shoes. I refused to look anyone in the face because I was too ashamed. When I was called to the back, I went alone. Mom didn't go with me. I don't remember if she just wasn't allowed or if she chose not to go. I remember some lady coming in the room saying something and reading off some rules to me. I also remember getting undressed and putting on some hospital gown. As I was lying on the table refusing to talk or even look at the people in the room with me, the Dr told me to relax. I stared at the bright light above my head…he murmured something and stuck something inside me…there was pulling…there was pain…there was misery…there was death. I cried, but not the body shaking, tear jerking type of cry. I just laid on the table and a few tears rolled down the side of my face. My baby was viciously stripped from me and the emptiness I felt consumed my being. I wanted to die with my baby. When I walked to the front of the office, I refused to look at anyone. How could I? I was a murderer. I allowed some strange man to rip my baby from my womb without even so much as a fight. On the way home no words were spoken. I curled up in the backseat, asked my baby that I would never hold to please forgive me, and cried myself to sleep. After that day the abortion was never spoken of again. I believe had I been given an option in the matter I would have chosen to keep my baby, but now I forever live with the fact that we killed my baby.

R.I.P to my baby boy or girl

This year you would have been 20 years old.

GEORGIA BOUND: As soon as school was over, mom told us that we would be moving to Georgia. She had been transferred to another base. I would be leaving my friends again and I was not happy about it. I wanted to stay in Florida and graduate with all my friends, but it wasn't going to happen. A few weeks later, we were on our way to Macon, GA. Mom had gotten transferred to Warner Robins AFB. In Macon we lived in some very nice apartments but the school I went to, Houston County High School, was actually in Warner Robbins. I was an 11th grader and didn't have very many friends nor was I interested in making new friends. I was not sure how long I would be at the school so making connections was not what I wanted to do. I can say I was pretty much a loner. The sexual abuse had not stopped. If anything my stepdad began to mess with me more because the opportunity was there more. There were times he checked me out early from school just to take me home and fondle me. I remember several times we would be driving the 45 minute drive from my school back to Macon and the entire time he would be feeling on my vagina with one hand while steering the car with the other. He had become a pro at humiliating me and victimizing me. Even during the time that I started working after school at Hardees he touched me. During the week, he was the designated one to pick me up and on the way home he often took the longer way because he used that opportunity to fondle me. I knew what was going to happen anytime he and I were home alone or alone in the car but I never said anything to mom about it again. I guess you can say that even though I hated this man, I accepted the abuse. I mean everything in my body hated him but my voice was lost and I believe he knew this. I honestly was in a place where I didn't care what happened to me anymore. Mom had never protected me, my stepfather continued to violate me, my real father didn't take me away and

I believed no one cared about me. So many times I just wanted to run away and never return. Well I got my opportunity later during my 11th grade year.

SAFE HAVEN: Mom had allowed me to get a part time job at Hardees and working at Hardees was great. I liked the people I worked with and it was my escape from the fighting between mom and my stepdad as well as the abuse. While working at Hardees I met this man who became my "safe haven". He worked at Hardees as well and he was always really nice to me. He trained me and looked out for me if I messed something up. The few times I wanted to quit because I messed up orders, he encouraged me to stay and stick it out. He always told me how beautiful I was. It was obvious that he had taken a liking to me. I was every bit of 15 or 16 and he was every bit of 24. I didn't care about the huge age difference and apparently neither did he because we eventually started dating. We only saw one another at work, but that was enough for me. I was young, dumb and really looking for someone to rescue me. Someone who would take me away from all the shit I was going through at home. I needed someone to be my safe haven and this man became that for me. He took my mind off the abuse and the fighting. He made me smile and during that time, I needed so badly to have a genuine smile. I never missed a day of work in anticipation of seeing him. Although we eventually moved from Macon to Warner Robins and I had to quit my job, he and I continued to talk and see each other. He would often come to the high school games and meet me there. We would leave out the game and sit in his car and talk and laugh. Here I was again, falling in love…so I thought. I truly believe I loved the possibility of this man rescuing me more than I believed in me loving him. One particular night mom and my stepdad were fussing and fighting while I was in the room getting ready to go to the school basketball game. Although the school was in walking distance and I walked to it everyday, my stepfather insisted on dropping me off to the game. When it was time for me to go, I couldn't get my seat belt on good before he started trying to fondle my private. Luckily the school was less than 2 minutes driving so as soon as he pulled up to the school, I hopped out and took off into the school gym. When I walked in, my boyfriend was already there waiting on me. I made sure my stepdad had left the parking lot and we walked to his car. As we were sitting in the car talking, he noticed that I was unusually quiet and asked me what was wrong. I told him nothing and asked him if he wanted to go somewhere. I told him I didn't care where; I just wanted to leave the school. That night we drove out to Macon back to his house where I ended up staying for almost a week. I didn't care about school, about if my mom was worried about me or not. As a matter of fact part of me never wanted to go back. I was tired of being violated and sexually abused, I was tired of seeing my stepdad beat the hell out of my mom, I was tired of cutting myself. I was tired and I thought this man was my way out. It wasn't until I had gotten word from a fellow classmate that the police were looking for him and me that I thought about going back home. Because we lived on base, when the man and I left the basketball game and drove through the security gate, our pictures were snapped. So the MP (Military Police) had his car information and our pictures. We were told that if I came back home by a certain date and time, no charges would be pressed against him. Reluctantly, I went back home but I honestly did not want to. I knew my boyfriend was much older than me and I didn't want him to get into trouble with the police. That was the ONLY reason I returned. Coming back home to the fighting between mom and my stepdad as well as the sexual abuse, sexual advances, sexual comments, mental abuse, emotional anguish and depression was overwhelming and my cutting became more frequent. After I came home, I was instructed not to talk to my boyfriend anymore, but I still did.

LEARNING TO DRIVE: As a teenager, the urge to learn to drive was overwhelming. I was in the 11th grade and wanted to have a car by the time I was a senior so I knew that I needed to learn how to drive. When I asked my mother about it, she automatically volunteered my stepfather to teach me. I wanted to decline the offer, but my urgency to drive outweighed my fear and reluctance. My first day of my driving lessons I really tried to push out the negative and enjoy the experience. But that was close to impossible. I remember one instance when my stepfather compared driving to sex. As I was learning the basics, I accidently pressed down on the gas pedal to hard and the car jerked forward. He put his hand on my right leg and began to rub the inside part of my thigh. As he was rubbing I tensed up and he told me to relax. He said that driving was just like having sex. You had to be gentle and take your time and ease into it. He told me to gently press down on the gas. Although my mind was telling me to slam on the gas and just run into oncoming traffic so I could hopefully die and be put out my misery, I did as I was told. I gently pressed on the gas and slowly moved forward. The driving/sex lesson lasted about 20 minutes before I just gave up all together. It was hard for me to concentrate on driving with his hand between my damn legs. After that day, I never cared to get behind a steering wheel again. The experience in itself ruined any exciting idea I had of driving and even today I don't care for driving.

WARD OF THE STATE OF GEORGIA: Every year since I started high school, in English class I had to write a term paper and every year I wrote on the one subject I knew the best: Child Sexual Abuse. My 11th grade year was no different. My topic that year would be the same as all the others. I remember going to the library and checking out about ten books. One night as I was sitting on the couch at my friend's house preparing the outline and doing my research, she asked me what I was doing my paper on and I told her. She looked at me funny and asked why that topic. It was then that I told her my secret of being sexually abused. Of course I made her swear not to say a word and of course she swore that she wouldn't. A few days later while in English class, I was standing in front of my fellow classmates reading my paper. The only difference this time was that I had written that I was being sexually abused instead of just writing about sexual abuse as a whole. In the previous years of writing about sexual abuse, never had I stated that I was being abused. I'm not sure what made me say that I was being abused this particular year. Maybe that was my cry for help. As I was reading my paper, I noticed my friend had gotten up and left out the class room. When she came back, as if on queue, the loudspeaker had come on and I was being called to the office. As soon as the voice on the loud speaker finished her request for me to come to counselor's office immediately, I looked at my friend who looked down at the floor. She could not even make eye contact with me and right then I knew she had told my secret. Although I was furious at her for telling my secret, there was a part of me that was relieved. Maybe now, since my entire family had failed me miserably, someone would protect me. As I walked to the counselor's office I was nervous, scared, and unsure. There was a part of me that was unsure of what I should say. I actually had a mental battle brewing in my head between telling the truth of my abuse or saying that it was all made up. I mean although I hated the abuse and the abuser, it had become my norm. I didn't know what would happen to him or my mother for that matter. I didn't know what would happen to me either but by the time I walked in the office, my mind was made up. I would tell what was happening to me and whatever happened just happened. The remaining of that day is in pieces in my head, but I do recall that I never went back to my class or my home that day. I don't know what was said to my mother or my stepfather. I just remember sitting in the counselor's office talking to the counselor and some other lady that I did not know. I don't remember what was sad to me or asked of me. Before school had even let out that day I was taken to a house that I had never been to before and when I walked inside it was full of young unfamiliar faces and their eyes were all glued on me. I was scared but refused to show it. I walked in and stood against the wall. My mind was in a million pieces and I wanted to go home. Later that night I found out that I was at the house of my new foster mom and all the young faces were her foster children. There had to have been about 6 of us in

all. I instantly felt uncomfortable and unwanted. I
had heard about foster care but never in a million
years had I expected to be in foster care. I never
thought I would become a foster kid…a ward of
the state. I only stayed at the house for few days
because it was temporary. The stay there was all a
blur to me. Now my second foster mother was a
nice elderly lady. She also had foster girls when I
arrived at her home but they were much younger
than me. They were about two and five years old.
My new foster mom was very sweet and I enjoyed
living with her. She didn't ask very many
questions, but she made it very clear to me that she
usually didn't take in teenagers because she didn't
want any problems. I promised not to be a
problem for her. She didn't live very far from the
high school I was attending so I walked to school
everyday. Although I was away from my family, I
don't remember feeling sad or remorseful. I was
not allowed to have any contact with my mother,
younger brother, or stepfather and had not spoken
to them in some weeks. I remember one time while
walking to school my mom had drove by me.
When she realized it was me that she passed by,
she turned around and threw some money out the
window to me and told me she loved me. She
didn't stop to talk or hug me or even ask if I was

ok. I wasn't sure how to respond, but I told her I loved her to, picked up the money and finished walking to school. I stayed with my second foster mom until the end of my 11th grade school year. I don't recall her name and I don't know what ever became of her or the little girls but I thank her for making an exception and taking me in. After the 11th grade, I remember a few times sitting in some room with my grandmother, some lady and my mother. I don't remember if that was my counseling or what but every time I left I seemed to feel worse that when I went in the room. I think this was because no one seemed to listen to me or even believe in me. My mom kept bringing up the fact that I ran away, but that's not why I was placed in foster care. I was not in foster care, living with complete strangers because I ran away from home. It was very much deeper than that but somehow mom saw it different. One day I recall sitting at the table and the lady telling me that I would be moving with my grandmother. Apparently my grandmother had become a foster parent and although I was still a ward of the state of Georgia, she would be my guardian. I was beyond happy. I was going to once again be with my family. Some weeks after that, I was on my way to the country to live with my Mommy. To this day, I still think about how even though I told the school counselor about my stepfather abusing me, I never went back to court. He never got prosecuted and he never went to jail. Yes, I was removed from the house but once again, he got off free. My faith in the system as I knew it was shattered to a point because I believed he should have went to jail for what he did to me. Instead, I was removed from the home as if I was the trouble maker and I stayed in the foster care system until the age of 17 when I aged out. To this day, I am listed as having been a ward of the state of Georgia.

HIGHSCHOOL SENIOR/HIGHSCHOOL MOM: My last year of high school I was living in the country with my grandmother and my cousins. My senior year was uneventful except when I became a mother to my oldest son. I was in a school where I only knew my cousin, a couple kids from church and the young man who became the father of my son. He and I met at the mall the summer before school started. Mom and my stepdad had eventually moved to the country as well but I didn't have very much contact with them except on holidays. I found out that mom had taken the early retirement from the military at 19 years in. Later she would blame her early retirement on me. As a senior, I eventually started working and my boyfriend and I began to get serious. I eventually became pregnant with my oldest and dropped out of high school. Of course dropping out was not what I planned, but that's how the cards fell. Did I have a say so, of course I did but I truly was not in the right frame of mind. By this time in my life all I wanted was someone…anyone to love me. When I found out I was pregnant, I remember making a call to my caseworker asking him when I would be able to move out of my grandmother's home. He informed me that at the age of 17, I was considered an adult and at that time I could leave. The day eventually came and it was quite a day to remember. The night before I went out with my boyfriend and decided not to come back home. We were at a hotel trying to decide who would call my mom and inform her that I was pregnant. He decided to make the call. When he called, I was terrified. Even though I no longer lived with my mom, I was still scared of her response. He made the call and I could hear her yelling and screaming at him. She was telling him how he had ruined my life and how she hated him. She wanted to speak with me, but I refused. After they got off the phone, I decided that I was not going back to my grandmother's home except to retrieve my clothes. The plan was for me to live with my boyfriend and his family. I made a call to my grandmother's and my cousin answered the phone. It was a Sunday so I knew they would be on their way to church. I told her to leave the window unlocked so I could get my clothes. She agreed. About twenty minutes later my boyfriend and I left the hotel and drove to my grandmother's house. When we pulled into the driveway, my grandmother's car was gone. I knocked at the door and when there was no answer we went around to the bedroom window, climbed in and began gathering up my clothes. While in the room, I heard my grandmother say, "Who is in there?" My boyfriend jumped out the window but I stayed inside. I yelled back to my grandmother that it was me and before I knew it, she had walked in the room with her gun pointed at me. She told me not to move and she was calling 911. My boyfriend was outside standing by his car. I could not believe that she was on the phone with the police telling them that I had broken in her house. I was furious. When the police got to the house, I told them that I lived there and how I knocked on the door and no one answered so I climbed in the window to get my clothes because I was moving out. The police officer asked my boyfriend if he went inside the house and he told them no. He knew that had he said yes, he would have gotten arrested. When the police officer asked my grandmother what she wanted him to do, she told him to take me to jail. I could not believe it. After all I had been through and now this. Instantly I felt as if, just like my mom, my grandmother had turned her back against me. I told her I could not go to jail for breaking into my own house and the officer agreed. Against my grandmother's wishes, they allowed me to get my clothes and we left. I remember while riding in the car to my boyfriend's house, I broke down in tears. I just felt as if everyone had turned their back on me and I was tired of it. My mother had turned her back on me by staying with my stepdad and not believing the abuse, my older brother had turned his back on me when he left home, my real father had turned his back on me by not rescuing me from the abuse, and now Mommy was turning her back on me by trying to get me arrested. I was a mess and that day I truly believed my entire family ad turned against me. The pain was unbearable because truth be told, I was the victim. That was the start of my victim mentality taking over.

Eventually my boyfriend's mother allowed me to live with them. She knew I was pregnant and welcomed me with open arms. She and I became quite close and I looked at her as my second mother. She looked at me as her daughter and although she was disappointed that we had gotten pregnant, she was one person who didn't turn her back on me. My nine months carrying my son was hard. It was hard to stay focused in school and eventually I just stopped going. It was hard being the 'black sheep' of the family, which is how I believed everyone, saw me. The pregnancy was rough but on October 3, 1995 my oldest son was born. I was the proudest mother alive and his father was the proudest father alive. It was our promise to never allow anything or anyone to hurt him and to be the very best parents we could be. The day my son was born was by far one of the happiest days of my life and four months afterwards, I married his father and we eventually moved to Tampa, Florida. Although we loved one another, we were young and at the time we did what we felt was right by our son. Neither one of us had come from families that gave us good examples of how to be a good husband & wife. His mother was a single parent and my mom and stepdad were far from good examples. We jumped in feet first and we both experienced the burden of bills, a baby, and simply not knowing what to do. Although I tried to put my own demons behind me, it was hard but I was determined to be the best wife I could. Sadly, it simply was not good enough. During our marriage there was infidelity, heartbreak and eventually some very hard decisions had to be made. Needless to say, our marriage lasted about two years.

BABY #2: While my first husband and I were going through our un-marital bliss, I began to speak again with the boyfriend I had back in the 8th grade. He and I had not spoken since my last year of high school. Not since he proposed to me, I accepted and eventually sent the ring back because I wanted to be with my son's father. I got back in touch with him and poured my heart out about how I was feeling and how I was so heartbroken over the state of my marriage to my son's father. He consoled me via the telephone and said things that made me feel whole again. He still professed his love for me after all those years and I could not deny that I felt something for him. Of course now looking back I know a lot of what I was feeling was due to what I was not getting at home. I felt lonely and abandoned by my son's father and this man filled that void for me at that time. I recall him and me speaking one night and he invited me to come visit him in Atlanta. He told me how he had his own place and how I could stay with him for a little while just to get away and clear my head. Without a second thought, I accepted the offer. In my mind at that time, getting away was what I needed. So I told my husband I was going to Georgia and I was taking our son with me. I recall him and my best friend trying to talk me out of it, but my mind had been made up. Later that week, my husband and my best friend took me and my son to the Greyhound bus station. My plan was to drop my son off in Savannah to his grandmother and continue on to Atlanta. We said our goodbyes and I was on my way. I stayed in Atlanta for about 3 months. During my stay, I was intimate and became pregnant with my daughter. Now let me say this, I am in no way proud of how things happened or the situation my daughter was conceived in, but it is what it is and I can not change the circumstances. I was young, dumb, and so very confused on life itself. My pregnancy was long, hard, and miserable. I was going through a divorce from my son's father, my daughter's father and I hated one another, and I was depressed. The hate between her father and I stemmed from me leaving Atlanta after I found out I was pregnant and his father accusing me of planting a baby on his son. The arguments, the screaming matches, the cursing, the tears, the hateful words spoken….all lead me to be severely depressed, losing weight, unable to eat and with my hair falling out. But God still blessed me to have a healthy daughter on November 18, 1998. My marriage to my son's father was over but not finalized in a court of law until December 1998. By this time, I was living back in Georgia in my own apartment, working at subway, and so very miserable. I had lost a total of 20 pounds while I was pregnant. I was 21 years old.

SECOND MARRIAGE: Shortly before my daughter was born, things between her father and I changed. I honestly was tired of the fighting back and forth. We both knew we wanted this baby and I was prepared to make things right between us. He eventually wanted to make things right too. After I had her, he came to where I was living to see her as well as to take pictures so he could show his parents who still believed she was not his, that she indeed was. She looked exactly like him and I dared him to say she was not his child when he came to visit. As expected, he could not. A few weeks after he came, his mother, father, and younger brother came…bearing gifts. I laugh now because it is so funny how some so called Christians will put you down, call you every name in the book, even refuse to walk on the same side of the street as you until they are proven wrong. In this situation, that's exactly what happened. His parents hated me with a passion because they did not believe I was carrying their grandchild. Even though their son KNEW I was pregnant from him. He KNEW because we planned to get pregnant. It was not until they saw her picture that they realized they had made fools of themselves. They had prejudged the situation and me and now needed to ease the situation over. In their eyes, that was to be done by showering my baby with gifts and becoming the doting grandparents literally overnight. I was furious and begged my grandmother (whom I was now staying with) not to allow them in her home. But my grandmother told me this.*"Regardless of what others may say about you, you know the truth. Let them come and be the grandparents to their grandchild. Don't block any blessings that may come along the way."* Those words alone have stuck with me for years. My grandmother had so much wisdom. Anyway, shortly after everyone saw my baby and things were mended, he and I made plans for me to move to Atlanta. I moved in December 1998 and on March 21, 1999 he and I were married. Our wedding was a home wedding. It was very small but special. I had not invited any of my family except my cousin who was my maid of honor but to my surprise my soon to be in-laws had. They had, without speaking to me first, invited my mother & stepfather. They even said something to my stepfather about giving me away. When I found out, I was furious. Not so much in them coming but in the idea of my stepfather giving me away. He could not beg for that privilege in my eyes. I did not ask him to give me away in my first marriage and I damned sure was not thinking about asking him to give me away in this marriage. He had taken enough from me over the years that he giving me away simply was not possible. In my second marriage, my three year old son gave me away and I could not have been more content. After we got married, we lived in his parent's basement. It was me, him, our daughter and my son. We were still both very young and although this was my second marriage, I was committed to making it work. I know that there was a part of me that loved him and I had always pictured myself as a wife so I believed I was ready to marry again. He on the other hand married because his father was a minister and it looked bad for us to be shacking up in his home. Although I didn't find out that was his reason for marrying me until many years later, it hurt to hear it all the same. My marriage to my second husband was rough. I began to have nightmares of my stepfather touching me and there were times I woke up fighting my ex-husband. His mother and I didn't really get along and he never seemed to stick up for me. Also my ex had a porn addiction and that tore into my self esteem daily. There were times that he preferred to watch porn or look at porn magazines than be intimate with me. His porn addiction desensitized him to love making, my feelings and even in pleasing me sexually. Sex eventually became all about him while I was left wondering what I was doing wrong. In addition to that, he was unhappy with my weight gain and made comments on a regular basis that would tear me up on the inside. I recall one day we were at the park with the children and he ran into one of his high school buddies. I was off a distance playing with the children and I had on a long blue dress. Later as we were leaving the park, he told me that he was embarrassed by me because his friend thought I was pregnant. I was devastated and was left thinking how can you love someone that you are embarrassed to be seen with. My ex-husband and I were living two different lives. He wanted to go out and party and be able to come in all times of the morning while I believed that behavior was for those who were single. He called me old fashioned and boring many many times. I was taking all this in, reliving my past, being hurt by how he treated me and boiling over with rage and eventually hate in my heart. The hurt grew into anger which grew into rage. I had so much rage that I began to fight my ex husband more times than I care to remember. It got to the point where I was so unhappy with my life, myself, my marriage, and him that any little thing he said would set me off on a tangent. We could be fussing and he would tell me the conversation was over and I would literally go in for the kill. My mindset was to hurt him physically the way I had been hurt emotionally for so many years by him and others. My hurt was so deeply rooted and deep inside I was broken. When I was in my fit of rage, I didn't care what I did or said to him. I didn't care that my children were watching near by and crying aloud. I didn't care if people heard me or even if the cops were called. It was like I was having an out of body experience and oftentimes afterwards, he would tell me that I wasn't the same person he married. He said the look in my eyes was like I was some demon possessed person. Today, I believe him. I didn't hate him, although I told him I did, but I hated the way he made me feel about myself. I hated that he didn't love me enough. I hated that my stepfather abused me. I hated that my mom did nothing. I hated that my family did nothing. All the hate and anger I held in for so many years was releasing itself and he was the recipient of that hate and anger. Outside of the fighting, we were struggling financially. We would get cars and have them repossessed. We would find places to stay just to get evicted months later. There was infidelity on his part which lead to distrust on my part. In spite of my fighting, I tried to reach out to him many times. I tried to connect with him emotionally by talking to him, writing letters, sending extremely long text messages and emails professing my love for him all to no avail. I only saw his wrong and spent so much time and energy trying to get him to see and fix his wrong. I refused to see my wrong because part of me believed I had a right to be mean and angry. His actions and words pushed me away and my actions and words pushed him away and it was a never-ending cycle. Eventually our marriage was on auto pilot. I'd gotten to the point where I was just tired. I was tired of crying, begging, pleading, fighting, searching, talking, and even living. I was unhappy and many times contemplated suicide to end it all. I felt as if I was a failure as a mother, a wife, and a person in general and truly was wasting space. I recall one morning after dropping the kids off to school I was sitting at a red light. My ex-husband and I had just had another argument and I had had enough. I had been crying all morning and had such heaviness on my heart. As the cars were driving in front of me, I just took my foot off the brake. I don't recall thinking about the outcome or my kids or anything. At that moment, I just needed to die. It was no longer a want for me but a need. As the car began to roll slowly into oncoming traffic I remember tears falling. I had truly lost all hope. As I willed myself to get hit by the cars and die, the car just stopped. The person behind me was leaning on their horn. Whatever trance I was in, was broken and when I regained my vision (because I truly was not seeing anything), I was stopped right under the red light. The car behind me honked their horn again and I wiped my eyes, stepped on the gas and drove away. The car that was behind me went around me and as they past me, I looked in their direction and the lady just smiled and kept on driving. I can say she saved my life, but deep down, I know it was a power much higher than what she possessed. It was God. I was angry with God that day. Why would HE not allow me to just die? Didn't He know I didn't want to live anymore? Couldn't HE see I was miserable? I was pissed but no matter how I was feeling, that day just wasn't my day to go.

BABY #3: Even though our marriage was messed up, we ended up getting pregnant again. It truly wasn't planned and I was shocked when I found out I was expecting. My ex-husband didn't want any more children but I had always wanted three. Many times I begged him for another, he would tell me no. Then he would come back and say that we could try for another. I remember many times getting all excited, thinking I was going to have another baby and maybe just maybe that would bring our marriage back together. We would have sex and at this time I didn't even care that there was no foreplay, no kissing, and no caressing. During the sex, all I thought about was getting pregnant and when he was getting ready to cum, he always pulled out. Each time, I was devastated and cried so hard. I asked him why he was playing these games with me. I asked why he would say one thing and do another. He always came back and said he didn't want any more kids. Needless to say when I found out I was pregnant, I was shocked and he was…well, not to happy. But I didn't care, I was finally going to have my third child and I did on May 22, 2005. He was the perfect little addition to our family and he immediately took up a space in my heart that was assigned just for him. Even after I had my son, my ex and I continued to fight, I was starting to drink, and the marriage was past going downhill, it was under ground by now. My ex and I lived together for 8 long, hard, mentally, emotionally, & physically draining years. It was not until 2007 that I made the decision to leave. We were due for eviction and I promised myself that if we actually got evicted from this place, then I would leave and find my own place. Well we did and I did. I found a 2 bedroom duplex around the corner from where we were and he moved in with his parents. There was a lot of drama with this move and him seeing the kids and helping me with them financially. Although I did not want to be a single parent to our children, I knew I needed a change. I was working at DeKalb Medical as a temp, about to get hired on permanent, when I made the decision that I needed to get far away.

MOVING TO TEXAS: I had made the decision to move to another state where I had absolutely no family. I spoke with my ex about the move, explained that I would be taking my two younger children with me. My oldest child was 12 and living with his father by this time. He agreed with the move. As a matter of fact he thought the move would be great for me so that I could start my life over. Not once did he object, ask about him seeing the children, or even asked me to stay for the sake of his relationship with his children. He helped me move the things that I did not sell into his parent's attic and he drove us to the airport. I had previously made arrangements with my longtime best friend who was living in Houston with her husband & children to stay with them until I could get on my feet. I was scared and did not know what to expect but I was determined to make a new life for myself. December 7, 2007 I left Atlanta, GA and arrived in Houston, TX. All we had were our suitcases and a few hundred dollars. When we touched down in Houston, a sense of happiness overcame me. I had never been to Houston but I was excited for the changes to come. I met up with my best friend. She and I had not seen one another since I left my first husband. Of course we had both grown but I was anxious to get to know her all over again. I was anxious to meet her family. I believed in my heart, that I had made the right decision. Once we got to her home, the children and I settled in, and my best friend and I began to reconnect. Her home was beautiful and she had done very well for herself. I was proud of her. But I have to be honest with myself; and this is something I never shared with anyone; there was a small part of me that held jealousy in my heart towards her. She had escaped an awful first marriage, remarried a great guy and had beautiful children. She was content in her life and most of all happy. I on the other hand was preparing for my second divorce and still had not figured out who Rhonda was. I was ashamed of my jealous feelings and tried so hard to shut them away. I didn't want that to come between our friendship. She and her husband made sure the kids and I were comfortable. I made it known that I would be paying them for allowing us to stay with them and when I got my taxes I did just that. Even though the Christmas holidays were fast approaching and I knew no one would be hiring, I still sent my resume out. In between the partying we did, I made sure to keep my focus on finding a job so that I could find a place to stay for the kids and I. January 14, 2008 I began working for a great company. My best friend started out taking me to work every morning and picking me up but eventually she informed me that I would have to start taking the bus. I never rode a city bus before so I had no idea on what I would have to do, but needless to say I did it. I had the help of her husband's cousin who was also living there and who I thought was taking a liking to me. He was a super sweet guy, but honestly was not my type and I had to stay focused on my goals. Anyway over time between going to work, going out, and trying to find my own place I noticed that my best friend had grown distant towards me. At least that is how it seemed. I soon grew tired of going out and drinking every week and started staying home more. I guess I realized that I was living a life that I simply was not about. Going out and drinking was not what I did and I honestly think I was just following the crowd so to speak. So like I said, I noticed she was growing distant from me…or perhaps we were growing distant from one another.

APPROVED FOR MY OWN: Although things seemed strained in the house, she still took me to go looking for places to live. I found one place that wasn't to far from her. It was a cute little two bedroom one & a half bath duplex. I put in my application, explained my situation to the landlord and within a week, I had been approved. I was so excited. I had no furniture, no beds, no dishes or pots and pans, but I had a place to call my own. I was overly excited. First I landed a great job and now I had the keys to my own place. I was on the right path. My best friend and her husband agreed to allow me and the children to stay with them a little while longer until I could get my lights and water on. At least that was the plan.

FRIENDSHIP GONE WRONG: As I stated earlier, I had noticed that our friendship seemed different. She seemed more stressed out and angry a lot of the time. It seemed as though everyone in the home was tiptoeing around the house so as not to piss her off. She didn't really talk to me about what was bothering her so I pretty much stayed to myself and tried to keep my kids in line. Just like she was frustrated, so was I. The kid's father was not sending me any money to help with them and he and I still argued whenever we spoke on the phone. I didn't have my own car and I was tired of having to ask for rides. One day I was home alone with all the kids (my two and her three). I was in my room while all the kids were in the kid's room.

I remember my daughter coming in the room crying because my best friend's kids would not play with her and she said they were mean towards her. This was not the first time she had come to me with this, I was already frustrated and so I told her and my son to just come in the room with me and don't play with them. I also made the comment that they didn't have to be mean to my kids. When my best friend came home, her daughter told her what I said and before I knew it, she was in a rage. She was yelling and screaming at me like I was a child. I was shocked because I didn't believe I had said anything wrong. We began to fuss and before I knew it, she told me to pack my things and get out her house. Where was I to go with my kids? Yes, we had our own place, but we had no running water, no food, no money, and no nothing. She didn't care; all she wanted was for us to get out. And so we did. I packed up all our things, I thanked her husband and her for allowing us to stay with them and I left. My two small children & I with about 4 suitcases walked out her house at about 9pm. Each of the kids was toting a bag and I was pulling the 2 larger suitcases. Although I had been to our new place once or twice, I could not remember exactly how to get there on foot but we walked anyway. It was a long, hot walk. I was hurt, pissed, and completely confused. I could not believe that the best friend I had since the 9th grade had kicked us out her home and turned her back on me. She and her husband knew it was dark, they knew we had no family, and they knew I had two small kids but not once did they offer to drop us off at our place. In my eyes, she had turned into the same type of people my family had turned into and I no longer wanted anything to do with her. She hurt me in the worst way by putting us out over something that could have been talked about and resolved. But her decision was made, and as I walked down the street I made my decision as well. She was cut out my life. On the way there two guys in a truck offered to give us a ride but I declined. I didn't know them and I couldn't take any chances. I was truly alone in this city that we now called home and it was me and my kids against the world. About halfway to the new house, after making a few wrong turns a lady pulled up along side us and asked if we were ok. I told her yes and continued to walk. She offered to give us a ride. I was tired, the children were barely making it, and so I accepted. I thought to myself that if she tried anything, I would fight until one of us was dead. I was on guard the entire time. She offered me the front seat, but I chose to stay in the back with the kids. I could not risk getting out the car and she driving off with my babies in the back seat. I told her where we were going and she happily took us to our new home. I thanked the lady, ushered the kids out the car and got out myself. I have no idea who this lady was to this day because she drove off into the night. Whoever she was, she had to have been sent by God. As the kids and I got in the house, we put all the bags in the front room and it was not until my son started crying for food that I realized we had not eaten dinner. It hit me that I had no food to give him and no money to buy food with. I got mad all over again, but refused to show it. I knew that at that moment all I had to depend on was me. I asked myself what I was going to do. I immediately started cursing myself in my mind. Maybe I should have begged my best friend to stay longer. Maybe I should not have ever left Atlanta. Maybe this was all wrong. But if it was, then why did God allow me to come? My mind was all over the place.

BEGGING: In realizing that my children had to eat, I had to make a tough decision in a matter of seconds. I was instantly put in a situation that called for desperate measures. After I calmed my son down, we left the house again. I remembered there was a corner store up the street so we walked to the store and stood outside. It was about five minutes before someone pulled up. It was a man of Mexican decent. As he was going inside to pay for his gas, I stopped him and asked him if he had some money I could have so that I could feed my babies. I thought he was going to say no, but he reached in his pocket and gave me two dollars. I thanked him and the kids and I walked to McDonalds across the street. That evening they ate a hamburger a piece and the guy behind the counter gave me a cup of water for them to share. I was starving myself, but I couldn't focus on that. As long as my babies had food, I would be ok. So instead I just thanked God for allowing my kids to eat and swallowed spit. After they ate, we left McDonalds and walked back home. We had to get up extra early the next morning because we had to walk to the daycare and I had to catch the bus to work. When we got back home, I took all the bags upstairs. Laid out clothes for the next day and laid out some of our clothes on the floor. The clothing on the floor was our makeshift bed. That night and many nights afterwards, we slept on those clothes and covered up with our jackets and coats. We could not bathe that evening because we had no running water. After the children were fast asleep,

I sat on the stairs and cried for what seemed like hours. I was so hurt by the events that had happened. Never in a million years could anyone have told me that I would have to stand outside and beg a stranger for money to feed my children. I felt low and ashamed. The next morning was one of many that became our weekly routine. We got up at 4am, got dressed, ate some toothpaste because we couldn't brush without water and began the long walk to the kid's daycare. The daycare opened up at 6am. We usually got there about 5:45am. I would sign them in, and leave out running to my bus stop which was about half a mile away. My bus came at 6:30am so I had to run/walk in order to make it on time. I knew that if I missed that bus, I would be late to work waiting on the next one. I usually got to work about 7:45 which gave me enough time to go in the restroom and freshen up. Eventually I was able to get my water on but while it was off, my darling neighbor allowed me to fill a bucket a couple times a day. That is how the kids and I washed up at night and flushed the toilet. I also was able to get a refrigerator with the help of my mother.

SUMMERTIME: School was about to let out in Houston but had already let out in Atlanta and my oldest son was coming to visit for the summer. I was excited because I had not seen him since I left Atlanta. I did not have transportation at the time so I had to ask a coworker if she could take me to pick him up from Hobby Airport. She agreed and we drove the 45 minute ride to get my son from the airport. I was so blessed to have had someone in my life that would help me at that time. I believe she was placed in my life by God. My son had grown so much and we were all so glad to see one another. I was glad to have a home for him to come to. Although I started out with nothing, by the time my son came I had a couch, chair, kitchen table, some pots & pans and some dishes. Some stuff I bought and some stuff was given to me by another coworker but regardless, I was feeling accomplished. Now I just needed a car because the long walks from the bus stop with two handfuls of groceries were brutal. But I did it for a long time. And on the days I needed to do heavy grocery shopping, I called a cab to pick us up. Likewise for the days that it rained heavy, I had to call a cab to take the kids to the daycare and to work. You can imagine how much money I spent on a cab some days. While my oldest son was visiting, we began to attend this church. I had not been to church in some time and it felt good to be back in the house of the Lord. It was very much needed for me at that time. Without a car the kids and I didn't do very much, but we enjoyed the company of one another. The summer came and went so fast and before I knew it, it was time for my son to fly back home. His departure was especially hard for my youngest son and equally hard for me.

BACK ON THE DATING SCENE: Once I felt as if I was getting my life back on track, I decided to start dating. Although I was legally married, I had no intentions on going back to Atlanta or my soon to be ex husband. We were not legally divorced yet because when I moved to Houston my main priority was not getting a divorce but finding a job, a place and getting my kids & I settled. Because I have been a wife since the age of 18, I had no idea how to "date" as an adult. I did not club or go to bars so I was unsure where or how I would meet anyone. I saw different commercials on TV about the different dating sites so I registered for some and eventually began conversing with men. Majority of the conversations were just phone conversations. Part of me was scared to meet men from online but another part of me knew that I would not meet a man any other way. Besides work and the grocery store and church, I didn't leave the house. Eventually I met a man whom I believed to be nice and respectable. We talked almost every day and I must say he was a smooth talker. He was very encouraging and seemed to be a decent man. The more we spoke, the more I began to trust him and one evening I invited him over. I asked him to arrive after the children were asleep because I was not ready to introduce another man into their lives right off. He understood completely. I remember putting the children to bed that evening feeling extremely nervous. I was nervous because I had not been alone in the company of a man other than my husband in 8 years. Although he and I spoke on a regular basis and had talked about almost everything under the sun, I was unsure of what to say to him in person. About 20 minutes after the children had fallen asleep; there was a knock at my door. I walked to the door wiping my sweating palms on my pants trying to pump myself up. I was telling myself that everything would go great. He and I would sit and talk and laugh then he would leave. I made sure to dress more conservative because I did not want to lead him on in any way. I did not want him to get any idea that I had invited him over for sex because that was by far the furthest thing on my mind. I just wanted to meet him in person and see if we clicked as well in person as we did over the phone. Just as I got to the door, he knocked again. I remember laughing to myself and thinking he was impatient but just as soon as I thought it, I pushed it out my head. I opened the door and before me stood a dark skinned man, about 6 ft tall with a muscular build a low hair cut and a very beautiful smile. I invited him in and as he walked past me, his cologne filled my nostrils. He sat on one end of the couch and I on the other. He could tell I was nervous and tried to break the silence by telling me how short I was. From that point on the laughter and conversation took off. He and I talked about everything, even some things we had previously spoken about over the phone but to me it seemed as if we were talking about everything for the very first time. I was totally comfortable and I was enjoying his company. Many times throughout our conversation, our eyes locked but I quickly shied away… but maybe not enough. I remember as we were talking about life in general, he leaned in and kissed me. I don't even recall him moving close enough to me to kiss me but he had slithered his way over. When he kissed me, I pulled back some and he grabbed me around my waist. In that instant, I knew this was not going to turn out good…and I was right. That night, the man that I had spoken to many times before, the man who shared his future dreams with me, the man who made me laugh and who portrayed himself to be kind, gentle, and respectable took me back to the 9th grade. That night he stole from me what was supposed to be mine to give. That night, I was raped…again. As this man who instantly turned into a monster pulled my clothes off me &thrust himself inside me I cried. I tried to push him off me but he was too strong. I began loudly begging him to stop, to please not do this to me but he ignored my pleas. I thought about my babies who were sleeping upstairs and I instantly shut my mouth. I could not risk my daughter coming downstairs and seeing this man raping me. So instead of screaming for help, I lay on the couch listening to his grunts and the feet on the couch scraping against the floor with each stroke. When he was finished, he got up, fixed his clothes and walked out my house with not even so much as a bye. I felt like a ragdoll. I felt like a piece of meat that was brutally beaten with a wooden mallet. I sat on the couch and cried. Why…How did I allow this to happen to me? After about 10 minutes passed, I managed to get up and lock my front door. I had not had sex with anyone since my husband and I split up so I was sore and I felt every inch of soreness between my legs as I wobbled upstairs to shower. As I was walking to the bathroom, I peeked in on my children and the tears would not stop. After much thought I decided not to press charges on the guy, mainly because I was scared. I didn't know what he was capable of, who he knew, and I was all alone in Houston. My mindset was "It happened; he didn't kill me, so I just needed to put it behind me and keep pushing forward." That is exactly what I did. I pushed the rape out my head and focused on my children. Needless to say, I was not in any rush to date anyone else. I deleted my page on the dating website, changed my number and moved on.

MY NEW CAR: As I stated earlier, because we didn't have a car, we either walked or caught the bus everywhere we went…rain or shine. Early in the mornings while it was still pitch black outside, 100 degree heat, and even with light rain falling, my kids and I walked the streets to get to our destinations. I remember one evening after work; I was walking to the daycare to pick the kids up and my mother had called me. She called to tell me that she had bought me a brand new Ford Focus. She had recently come into $500 thousand dollars from an accident she had on her job. I was ecstatic. I was so tired of walking and I had been praying to God for some type of transportation. As she was telling me about the car, she began to tell me that in order for me to get the car, there were some things I needed to do first. One of those things was I needed to send her a thousand dollars as a down payment for the car. Then I needed to of course make arrangements to fly the kids and I out to Florida to pick up the car. When I came to pick up the car, I needed to come with an additional thousand dollars. Then once I got the car, I had to make monthly payments to her until the car was paid in full. Although I thought her stipulations were steep, I agreed to them. I needed a car and if that's what I had to do to get one, I would do it. The next day after work, I received another call from my mother speaking about the car. Even though she stressed how this car was from her to me, it seemed as if her husband was calling the shots. Before I knew it, he was on the other line. I had no relationship with this man. Since I aged out of foster care, I stopped calling him dad and began to call him by his first name. I had no desire to speak with him, but yet, he was on my phone giving me all these rules about the car. I immediately became furious and one word led to another and before I know it, I was telling him to get off my phone because I had absolutely nothing to say to him…ever! I hung up on him. The next day after work, I called my mother back to apologize to her husband. As much as I despised him, I needed to humble myself because I knew that I needed transportation. It would be getting cold soon, and I did not want to have to walk in the cold with my children. When she got on the phone, she informed me that her husband felt I had not sacrificed enough therefore she would not be giving me the car. I was instantly livid. Not so much at the decision that was made because truthfully it was her money to do as she pleased but I was livid at the audacity of that man to say I had not sacrificed enough. I quickly reminded her that it was me who was walking in the dark, rain, and heat with my children. It was me who was miles away from my family because although I made the ultimate decision she constantly kept telling me not to move back to the country where my grandmother was because the family would suck me dry of money. It was me who was taking care of these kids by my self. I felt that I had sacrificed more than enough and I told her so. She told me that in a few months, if they felt I had sacrificed more then she would possibly give me the car. I began to cry and I asked myself how could a mother be so cruel hearted? I told her that she could keep the car because God would provide for me. August of 2008, I got my car. A coworker's father took me to Planet Ford and I was able to buy a 2003 Ford Taurus. It was not brand new like the Ford Focus my mother teased me with, but it was mine that I bought with my money and no crazy stipulations attached. Needless to say, I was extremely proud of myself. God had provided for my family and me once again. No more did we have to walk the dark streets to daycare and bus stops. No more did we have to walk in the rain and heat. No more did I have to walk constantly looking over my shoulder for fear of someone attacking us. No more did I need to rehearse the plan with my daughter if someone did attack us while we walked.

OUR FIRST HURRICANE: Shortly after God blessed us with our own car, we faced another challenge. This particular challenge was Mother Nature…this challenge was Hurricane Ike. I had never been in a hurricane before so I was totally unprepared as to what to expect. I kept watching the news for shelter locations just in case the kids and I had to leave our home. I made sure to stock up on water and food that did not need to be cooked. As the hurricane was settling in, I remember tucking the children in bed, saying a prayer for protection over us and going to bed myself. Surprisingly, we slept through the hurricane. The next morning I got up, checked on the children and the car and breathed a sigh of relief. All was well. The lights were off and I honestly expected the lights to come back on during the day. I also expected for our life to carry on as it had Pre Hurricane Ike, but I was so wrong. My daughter's school and my son's daycare were closed for almost a week. I missed several days of work due to not having anyone to watch the children. On top of that, day 3 had come along and we still were without lights. I had a BBQ grill and was able to grill up some meat; the rest of the food had to be thrown away. By day 5, food was very skimpy as well as money. After speaking with my neighbor, the kids and I went to a church to get some military rations. We must have eaten that for about another week. Due to the hurricane, the government was allowing people to get emergency food stamps. Luckily, I was able to apply for and get the food stamps and just in time too because shortly afterwards, the lights came back on and I was able to replace the food I had thrown away. Although we had survived our first hurricane, money was extremely tight. During the Hurricane, we spent quite a bit on eating out and before I knew it, money for bills was spent. By November, I began to receive disconnection notices for water & lights. I knew I did not have the money to pay almost 3 months of overdue bills at once, so I tried to make arrangements. Not only was I behind in my utilities but also in my rent. It was not until one day after work when I came home to an eviction notice pinned on the front door that I broke down. I knew that I had to try and get the money up somehow, but had no idea how. Reluctantly, I called my mother and asked for help. She and my stepfather spoke with my landlord and from my understanding made an agreement with the landlord to pay the rent. I was under the impression that they were going to send the landlord a check for the rent. Well by the December, I received a call from the landlord who informed me I had to be out his place. He had never received any money from my mother and her husband. The landlord told me that if I was out by the end of December, then he would not take me to court. I was naïve to the landlord/tenant rules and so I agreed to leave his property. Within the next week or so, our things were packed and my neighbor across the street helped me move our things into a storage unit. As I walked from truck to storage unit with bags of clothes, pots & pans, and toys I thought to myself, "What now?" That day, I had no plan in place. I did not know where we would go, where we would sleep, or what we would eat. All I knew was that, somehow I had messed up not just my life, but the life of my children. I knew that I had failed them as a mother. Here I was in a state with two small kids, no place to go, no money, and broken. I prayed to God to please make a way…any way. I knew that if anyone could get me out of this mess I created, it could only be him.

NOWHERE TO GO: After we got all our things in the storage, the kids and I drove around for a while and ended up at McDonalds. As the kids were happily eating their dollar fries, laughing and joking around it was evident that they had no idea that they were homeless with nowhere to go. But I knew better and the weight on my shoulders was heavier than a ton of bricks. I remember sitting at the table looking up shelters on my cell phone. As I was looking, I was praying that somehow something would come up so that the kids and I didn't have to go to a shelter. But as I dialed the number to Star of Hope, and the lady answered I knew that the "something" I prayed for would not come forth. By the time I finished speaking with the lady at the shelter, it had really hit me that I was homeless with my children. Never in my life had I been homeless with nowhere to go. Even though I had lost apartments in the past while living in Georgia, I always had a sure place to go with my children. As I rushed the kids to finish eating, I continued to pray to God to not make me go to a shelter. At that time, my mindset was that a homeless shelter was for people who did not work and who had absolutely nothing. When I thought about homeless, I thought about the men and women I saw walking the street with dirty clothes, torn shoes, and dirty hair. In my mind at that time, I was above those types of people. In my mind, I did not belong in a shelter. Well God had a lesson to teach me and my lesson started at Star of Hope.

When we got to the shelter, I parked my car and reluctantly walked in the shelter holding my kid's hands extremely tight. This is how shallow my thinking was: When I walked in the shelter I told the lady behind the glass that I needed a room for my children and me. I actually expected her to give me a room that was made up like a hotel room. I expected to have my own shower, my own comfortable bed and my own privacy. After she looked at me in a manner as if she was questioning who I was, she asked me if I was already on the list. I told her no, I was not on a list but I had just called about 30 minutes ago and was told to come down to the shelter. She then explained to me that since I was not already on the list for a space, that my children and I had to wait in the lobby until a certain time. After that time we would be allowed to go in the main area and get some food. After that, if there was room then we could get a cot and sleep in the main area with hundreds of other families. I was devastated. I did not want to sleep in a room with other homeless people. I did not want to eat with other homeless people. Somehow even though I was homeless too, I looked my nose down on the homeless. The lady interrupted my thoughts and told me that if I was going to stay for dinner, I needed to sign in. I knew my children needed to eat. My son had begun to whine because he was hungry, so I had no choice. I did as I was told and found a seat in the corner with my children. As I sat quietly, I watched people coming and going. I saw families…husbands, wives, and children. I saw teenage girls with babies. I saw handicapped people. I saw elderly people. I saw a woman with her husband who was wearing a jacket that said I am a Veteran. Right then, God began to deal with me and it dawned on me that I was no different than the same people I previously looked down on. I immediately felt horrible. I felt as though the people who walked pass me did not deserve to be in the same room with someone like me. They deserved better and I asked God to forgive me. Who was I? How dare I look down on someone as if I am better when we are in the same boat? I was just as homeless as they were and furthermore, they probably had a better plan about their life than I did about mine at that very moment. By the time I finished beating myself up, it was time for dinner. The children and I fell in line behind the others to be served. It was not until I sat down at the table that I realized I was starved. I had not eaten anything all day. I fed the children and ate myself then went back to the waiting room. We waited about another hour before the lady came and told us there was no space for any more people. Me, the kids, and about 30 more people truly had no where to go. It hit me that we couldn't even stay at the shelter with the people I thought I was better than. So in reality they were better off than me because at least they had a place to lay their head that night whereas the children and I had nowhere. I remember calling the children's father and crying on the phone telling him what happened and that we had nowhere to go and no money. I remember his exact words because they will forever be stuck in my head. He said, "You mean to tell me you moved all the way to Texas just to end up homeless?" I was instantly furious and began to curse him out. I did not care who heard me. I hated him with a passion and at the moment, I truly wanted to kill him. I remember thinking that had he been the husband he was supposed to be, I would not even be in Texas. I was so mad that I stared to cry and the madder I got, the harder I cried. I hung up on him and took the kids to the car. The plan was to sleep in the car and in the morning look for another shelter. I laid my son down in the back seat and told my daughter to get in the front seat and let it back. I covered them up and then I got in the drivers seat and laid my seat back as well. Although I was beyond tired, I was not able to sleep. We were in the parking lot of the Star of Hope and I was scared that something could happen. I remember praying and asking God to protect us from any hurt, harm, or danger. About 30 minutes later, the children's father called back and told me his cousin would be calling me. His cousin and his wife had agreed to allow the kids and me to stay with them until I found another place. As soon as he hung up, the phone rang again and it was his cousin. I think he and I had met only once in the 8 yrs I was with my children's father. He told me that the children and I could stay with him and his wife until I found a place and gave me directions to his home. I was beyond grateful. I cried because even though I was very self centered and mean earlier in my thoughts towards other homeless people, God still provided for me and the children. He allowed a stranger, in a sense, to take us in. Instead of that man and his wife looking down their nose at me (as I had done earlier), he allowed them to have compassion for me. God was definitely beginning to deal with me….and I needed to be dealt with.

After I got off the phone with the cousin, I drove to their home, thanked them both once again and thanked God for being the provider that He is. It was ONLY because of Him that the children and I did not have to sleep in a car. Now although we were still considered homeless (not having our own home), God did not look his nose down at me. Instead he blessed us. We stayed with the cousin and the wife until I got my taxes in February. Once I got my taxes, I was able to find the children and me a two bedroom, two bath apartment. Once again, God stepped in and worked it all out for us.

When all you know is anger, hurt, & rage, that is who you allow yourself to become.

Part 3: Healing the RAGE

DEALING WITH ME: After we moved from the cousin's home into our own home we tried to pull our lives back together. I eventually tried the dating thing again making sure to proceed with caution. As expected, I ran into a couple more frogs but I didn't allow that to discourage me. There was the one guy who I found out was a married man, the other guy who was just a liar and a cheat about everything, and then another guy who didn't like children. For the life of me, I could not understand why I was attracted to these types of men. I was confused on IF I was even supposed to live my life in peace and be happy. That was one of the main reasons I moved to Houston in the first place….to find peace & happiness. Well it was after a year long relationship had ended with one man that I realized something very important was missing from my life. I realized that I would never be able to have a happy relationship with anyone as long as I continued to hold on to and carry what felt like a 50 ton weight of all my past hurt and pain. I realized that I had not properly dealt with the things of my past that still haunted me. Things like the sexual abuse, like my mother not protecting me, like the rapes, and the feeling of being unloved and unwanted. I realized that I needed to learn how to forgive and move on forward with my life so that I could accomplish my goals. It was after that last relationship that I promised myself I would not date or even talk to another man until I was free from the pain that drowned me. I knew that I needed to do the required work in order to heal properly from all that I was carrying inside me. I knew that I needed to have a heart to heart with God and I knew that if I did not do it right then, I never would. I was tired of fussing back and forth with mom about the abuse. I was tired of crying at night because she still didn't believe me. I was tired of writing down what happened over and over as if I was trying to prove to myself what I knew in my heart was true. I was tired of the screaming matches with my children's father. I was tired of crying myself to sleep at night because I believed I had no one to love me and was unworthy of love. I was tired of not loving myself properly. I was tired of looking at myself in disgust. I was tired of the hurt and the anger boiling up inside me until I vomited blood. I was tired of popping pain pills just to sleep at night or make myself numb to life. I was tired and needed to find a way to allow the peace &

happiness I longed for in my life to find me. That way was through strengthening my relationship with the Most High and looking deep within myself and facing my truth. I had to face that I was holding everyone who came into contact with me responsible for my hurt and pain. I was blaming the world for my misery and in the process, I was dying inside. I had to accept the fact that I was not happy with myself and who I had allowed my past to turn me into. To be truthful, I was an angry, hurt, woman who walked with a chip on her shoulder and in constant rage. I needed healing and I had to admit that fact to myself first before I could even go to the Most High. I refused to go to Him half stepping. I promised myself that I would put it all out on the table and with His help; I would begin my healing journey. And that's exactly what I did. It's never easy to come face to face with your own demons. It surely was not easy for me, but it was something I had to do because I knew that if I did not, then I would eventually kill myself. Even though I got up every morning, went to work, came home, cooked for my kids and prepared for the next work day, everyday was a battle for me. Every night I had the conversation with myself of to kill or not to kill.

MY HEALING JOURNEY: In making the final decision to start my healing process, I realized that I had allowed my past to determine my future. I allowed it to dictate my words, my actions, and my thoughts. I had allowed it to invade my self esteem and beat me down in the worst way. Although I knew I was the victim of the abuse and rapes I endured, and although I had healed physically, I knew that I had not healed emotionally or mentally. One day while the kids were taking a nap, I went into my closet and began to listen to some gospel music. As the music moved me, I began to pray and ask the Most High to take my pain away. I began to ask Him to heal me and to be my peace. From growing up in the church I had always heard the older generation recite *Isaiah 53:5.*

Isaiah 53:3

But He was wounded for our transgressions; He was bruised for our iniquities: The chastisement for our peace was upon Him, and by His stripes we are healed.

It was the last part that stuck out to me…***<u>By His stripes we are healed</u>***. I began to believe that this was not talking about just physical healing but any type of healing. And so in my believing I cried for emotional healing. I begged for mental healing and I trusted and believed in the Most High to heal me. His Word told me to ASK and so I asked as though my life depended on it…because truly, it did. As I was crying out to the Lord, pouring my broken heart and bruised soul out to Him, the word FORGIVENESS popped in my head. Just as quickly as it popped in, I pushed it out. I told the Lord, I didn't need forgiveness; I needed healing but that word continued to come in my head. It was so constant that I could not continue to ignore it. I assumed the Most High was telling me that in order for me to get healing; I had to ask for forgiveness. So I began to ask for forgiveness of all the things I had done wrong. I was in my closet for about an hour or so begging for forgiveness and healing. I was willing to do what ever the Most High said I needed to do in order to live the life I believed I deserved. He said forgiveness, so I asked for forgiveness. By the time I came out the closet, I was tired and cried out but I was confident that God was working on my behalf. It was not until some time later as I was writing in my journal that it hit me…God was not telling me to ask for forgiveness, He was telling me to forgive. Well when that came to me, I immediately went into defense mode. I was asking God why I had to forgive. I was the VICTIM! I was the one who had been abused and raped! Why was He telling me to forgive? My stepfather had never even admitted what he did much less apologized for doing it. And mom, she still believed him over me!! I was not trying to hear anything about forgiving anyone because I believed in my heart that I deserved to be angry. As I was sitting in my room fuming, God brought back to my remembrance how I had said I was willing to do whatever He said I needed to do. He also brought to my remembrance that I too was a sinner and had done some things that He was not happy about. He reminded me that I was to forgive those who trespass against me by bringing the scripture Matthew 6:14-15 to my remembrance.

Matthew 6:14-15

For if you forgive men their trespasses, your heavenly Father will also forgive you. But if you do not forgive men their trespasses, neither will your Father forgive your trespasses.

As I was trying to fathom the idea of forgiving my abuser, my rapists, my mother, and everyone else in my family who did not protect me, I began to cry. How could I forgive someone who stole my innocence from me? How could I forgive the one who was supposed to protect me but did not? I knew that this healing journey was going to be long and hard but I also knew deep in my soul, no matter how hard it would be, it was a journey that I needed to take in order to be whole. And so, it began with me writing letters. The idea of writing a letter to the one who hurt me came from a talk show. I want to say it was on Oprah but the truth is, I don't recall whose talk show it was. But I do recall the person talking about how writing out what you wanted to say to the person and being totally honest with them could be helpful in your healing. So, I began to write. That night, I wrote a letter to my stepfather telling him how it made me feel when he touched me inappropriately , how it distorted my trust in men, how it made me feel dirty and ashamed. How I hated him at one point in my life and how my childhood and early adulthood was ruined because of what he did. I shared with him the pain I carried daily, the attempted suicides, the desire to die just to end the hurt I carried so deeply. I told him that I did not know why he chose me to do what he did but I suspect because it may have happened to him and because he had no true connection to me because I was not his biological daughter. I told him that even though what he did to me was meant for no good, God was going to turn it around for some good and I would be blessed. I told him that I forgave him and that if he sincerely asked God for forgiveness, He would forgive him as well. By the end of this 15 page letter, I was crying tears of pain. This was the pain and confusion that I had held inside me for so many years. This was the pain and anger I allowed to rule my life. This was the pain and rage I almost allowed to take my life. After I finally finished writing, I folded the letter, put it in an envelope, sealed it and set it in my bible. I then proceeded to write my mother's letter. Her letter was as long if not longer than my stepfather's but I made sure to say everything my heart had on it to say. And at the end, I told her that I forgave her and I meant it. My letter writing lasted for about a week and a half. I wrote letters to everyone…some no more than a page and some considerably longer. I even wrote a letter to myself because I realized that in holding onto my hurt, anger, pain, and rage that I had hurt myself and needed to truthfully forgive myself. And in understanding that I had hurt myself, I could not hide the truth that I had hurt others. I knew that I had hurt my children and my ex husbands, and even some close friends with my words and my actions so I wrote letters to them asking for their forgiveness. For me, the letter writing was a great release on my soul. It allowed me to say the things that I may have never said and to say it without the hatred and anger. It allowed me to get everything out without being rushed, dismissed, or interrupted. Now, I wish I could say that after writing the letters to those who hurt me I was able to simply move on and forget the past, but that would be a lie. I still battled nightmares, feelings of unworthiness and even disappointment, but the rage deep inside my heart was lifted. I understood that it was not up to me to punish anyone for the things they did to me. It was my responsibility to forgive them and to pray for them…not for their peace of mind, but for my own. As time went by, I was able to acknowledge what had happened to me, accept the truth for what it was and today I am still advancing through it all. Healing does not happen over night. I mean the hurt and rage did not build up over night, it had been brewing for many years. The good thing is, at the end of every day, I know I am one step closer to total restoration. I know that God is my healer and during the days where I still get weak in my flesh and want to lash out, He is my strength.

Psalms 28:7

The Lord is my strength and my shield; my heart trusted in him, and I am helped; therefore my heart greatly rejoiceth; and with my song will I praise Him.

Part 4: A NEW Me

Today, I can tell my story of survival because I am a SURVIVOR!! And in my telling it, I no longer have to tell it through the eyes of who I was, how I portrayed myself and how I allowed people to treat me…as the victim. I no longer try to figure out why mom chose to handle my sexual abuse in the manner she did, nor why my stepfather refused to fight his temptations of touching me inappropriately. I stopped wondering if my rapists were sorry or ashamed of their actions or why no one in my family came to my rescue. Now I just continue to look to the Most High for guidance and direction. I know that in the end He gets the glory for it all. I look at where I was in life at one time…broken, hurt, homeless, angry…and the list goes on. Then I look at where I am in life today…healed, happy, married to a wonderful man who loves me despite my past, raising wonderful children, and in a position to help other women understand the importance of beginning their own healing journey. This road was not easy for me by any means and it's not over. Day by day I continue to push forward. I still have a strained relationship with my mother but I have accepted it for what it is. I have stopped trying to be who she wants me to be and I have found out who I am called to be and strive to be the best. Today, I love me more than I used to. I respect me and I am no longer ashamed of the things I have endured. I no longer have to cut myself or fight my husband, or drink my sorrows away. I have a voice!! Today when I look in the mirror, all I can say is Thank You Abba (Father)!! It is truly because of whom YOU are that I AM because had it been left up to me, I probably would not be here to write this book. I understand today that I was allowed to live and not die because there is a divine purpose for me. There were many times in my life that I begged for death, yes, I was just that miserable and depressed and lost. But the Most High was not having it. He is the giver & taker of life itself and today I am more than thankful that He has given me life and more abundantly so. I have an assignment in this life and until that assignment is complete I'll be right here. I understand wholeheartedly when the older generation says Satan is out to kill, steal, and destroy because I was his target and he almost succeeded. He played on my sexual abuse and my rapes and my failed marriages and tried to take me out. He put thoughts in my head telling me that I was no one important, nothing, used and abused up and that no man would want me. He put on my heart that my life was worthless, but after I called out to God I was able to see that those were just tricks of the trade. Satan has no power over me because I am a child of the Most High. He set out to demolish me……..BUT GOD!!!

My Inspiration to YOU:

Today is a new day…every day is a new day and no matter what pain, hurt, anger, and even rage that you are carrying, all you have to do is give it to the Most High and allow Him to work on your behalf. He desires you to be happy, healthy (mentally, emotionally, physically, and spiritually) and healed!!! We as a people must realize that holding on to anger and hurt only hurts us more. It stops us from living a healthy life and of course we know that hurt people hurt people. No matter what you must do in order to begin your healing process…I urge you to DO IT!!! It could be writing letters, seeking a counselor, writing in a journal, joining a support group or crying out to the Most High. No matter what your method is, it is yours and it is important. No one person has all the answers or the sure fire way for another to heal but I stand by a few things in any healing process and they are:

Prepare Yourself

Acknowledge the Hurt

Accept the Hurt

Advance through the Hurt.

I believe one hundred percent that those four steps will help you claim survivorship. *(You can get more information about those steps in my booklet "Heal Your Hurt" which is to be released soon)* I know that I could not have done this alone and neither can you. I also know that even though I had many people encouraging me and praying for me that MY HEALING was because of the Most High's grace and mercy and so is yours. He obviously saw something in me to "save" me from myself and He sees something in you. When I desired peace, He showed me that He was my peace and He is yours. When I was looking to man to make me whole and to love me as I desired to be loved, God showed me that I was already whole in Him and so are you. He showed me that only He could love me unconditionally and only He can love you unconditionally. Just like you, there were many many nights that I cried, but the Most High God assured me that my JOY was coming in the morning as long as I trusted and depended on Him. As long as I kept my heart on Him and not on the situation or the circumstance, then I would be able to *Heal the Rage Within* and so will you.

Psalm 30:5

--Weeping may endure for a night, but JOY cometh in the morning.

About the Author

Yuoranda Walker is the wife and mother to a wonderful & caring husband and three wonderful children. She resides in Houston, TX where she enjoys writing, reading, and spending time with family, friends, and her two Pitt Bulls, Maxie & Colby. Although *Healing the Rage Within* is her first full book, it is not her first literary piece. She had the pleasure of joining eleven other women in the sharing of their true life stories in the book titled, *The Journey*, which is available on Amazon. Yuoranda has always had a passion for writing and the completion of her first book is a great accomplishment for her and opens the pathway to many more books in the future.

In addition to being a wife, mother, & an author, Yuoranda is also Survivor & Founder of Healing R.A.G.E. (*R*aped & *A*bused *G*irls *E*verywhere) which is a local organization dedicated to the healing & healthy living of women who have been abused & raped. She started her organization in November 2011 as a way to reach out & encourage women survivors to start their healing journey. She is very passionate about the long term effects of not dealing with the abuse and/or rape and has coined the phrase *Heal Your Hurt.*

For more information about **Healing R.A.G.E.** please visit www.healingrage.org.

Look for these UPCOMING book releases by Yuoranda Walker!

- ❖ Heal Your Hurt ~ A Four Step Guide to Starting Your Personal Healing Journey (Workbook)
- ❖ Falling in Love with Yourself ~ A 30 Day Inspirational Journey to Loving YOU
- ❖ Beyond Broken

NOTES

NOTES

NOTES

Made in the USA
Monee, IL
08 March 2025